H2O A JOURNEY OF FAITH

H2O A JOURNEY OF FAITH

Group Leader's Guide

Ross Brodfuehrer

Standard
PUBLISHING
Bringing The Word to Life

Cincinnati, Ohio

© City on a Hill Productions™ Inc. 2006, as licensed to Standard Publishing, an unincorporated division of Standex International Corporation. All rights reserved. No part of this book may be reproduced in any form—except for brief quotations in review—without permission of the publisher.

All Scripture quotations, unless otherwise indicated, are from the HOLY BIBLE, *NEW INTERNATIONAL VERSION*®. *NIV*®. Copyright © 1973, 1978, 1984 by International Bible Society. Used by permission of Zondervan. All rights reserved.

Where indicated, Scripture is taken from the following versions and used by permission: Scripture quotations marked *(TLB)* are taken from *The Living Bible*. Copyright © 1971 by Tyndale House Publishers Inc., Wheaton, IL 60189. Used by permission. All rights reserved. Scripture quotations marked *(NCV)* are taken from the *New Century Version*®. Copyright © 1987, 1988, 1991 by Word Publishing, a division of Thomas Nelson Inc. Used by permission. All rights reserved. Scripture quotations marked *(The Message)* are taken from *The Message,* by Eugene H. Peterson. Copyright © 1993, 1994, 1995, 1996, 2000, 2001, 2002 by NavPress Publishing Group. Used by permission. All rights reserved. Scripture quotations marked *(NLT)* are taken from the Holy Bible, *New Living Translation*. Copyright © 1996 by Tyndale House Publishers Inc., Wheaton, IL 60189. Used by permission. All rights reserved. Scripture quotations marked *(NIRV)* are taken from the HOLY BIBLE, NEW INTERNATIONAL READER'S VERSION™. Copyright © 1995, 1996, 1998 by International Bible Society. Used by permission of Zondervan. All rights reserved. Scripture quotations marked *(CEV)* are taken from the *Contemporary English Version*. Copyright © 1991, 1992, 1995 by American Bible Society. Used by permission. All rights reserved.

MERE CHRISTIANITY by C. S. Lewis copyright © C.S. Lewis Pte. Ltd. 1942, 1943, 1944, 1952.
Extract reprinted by permission.

ISBN: 0-7847-1974-8
13 12 11 10 09 08 07 06   9 8 7 6 5 4 3 2 1

CONTENTS

INTRODUCTION 7

EPISODE 01 ▶ **Thirsty** 19

EPISODE 02 ▶ **Polluted** 29

EPISODE 03 ▶ **Source** 39

EPISODE 04 ▶ **Pure** 49

EPISODE 05 ▶ **Mirage** 57

EPISODE 06 ▶ **Drowning** 65

EPISODE 07 ▶ **Drink** 73

EPISODE 08 ▶ **Clean** 81

EPISODE 09 ▶ **Vapor** 87

EPISODE 10 ▶ **The River** 95

H20 PARTY 103

Introduction

WHAT IS H2O?

H2O is water, of course!

But beyond the scientific formula, H2O is an evocative, DVD-driven, group-oriented, ten-week experience designed to create an atmosphere in which nonbelievers feel comfortable openly considering—and maybe even drinking of—the living water, Jesus Christ.

Here's the idea: a small team of Christ-followers commit to hosting an H2O series in one of their homes. They ask unchurched friends and family to come watch and discuss the concepts conveyed in some intriguing DVDs that illustrate what Jesus is all about.

At each gathering, those who take part enjoy a meal together. Why a meal? Remember Acts 2? The early believers broke bread in each other's homes. Eating together is a powerful way to break down barriers and help people feel at home.

After dinner, the leader plays a 20–30 minute DVD episode of H2O. Here's where the good stuff really begins! Each segment unfolds a dramatic story coupled with insightful teaching presented in a fast-paced, image-driven fashion. The format is a little hard to describe. You just have to see it to appreciate it. Go ahead and check out a couple of episodes and see what you think!

After viewing the DVD, the leader facilitates an open discussion around the ideas communicated in the presentation. The leader doesn't have to be a teacher. In fact, it's better if the leader does *not* teach! The leader should facilitate conversation—keep the discussion moving and make sure the atmosphere is open, nonjudgmental, and conversational. Let the Holy Spirit and the DVD do the teaching!

Facilitating discussion will give people a chance to think through—and talk through—their responses to the person and message of Jesus. Participants remember better and are changed more by what they themselves say than what you say. Each discussion lasts 30–40 minutes.

Each episode takes the participants one step further on a carefully crafted tour of the person and purpose of Christ. H20 contains ten episodes, so that's ten weeks, plus an End-of-H20 celebration. An Overnight Getaway in the middle of the study, at which you view episodes 6 and 7, can be a powerful time for the group to connect and make decisions. Adding this all up, you'll have eight home sessions, an overnight getaway, plus a final party.

Also included is an extra DVD called *Storm*, which contains ten teaching segments, set in a coffeehouse environment, that deal with the common objections and questions that so often arise in a group like this. That means that you don't have to have all the answers! You can simply loan out *Storm* to anyone struggling with tough questions. The following topics are included on *Storm:*

1. Questions About God
2. Questions About Creation
3. Questions About the Bible
4. Questions About Jesus (part 1)
5. Questions About Jesus (part 2)
6. Questions About Suffering
7. Questions About Prayer
8. Questions About Satan
9. Questions About Afterlife
10. Questions About Questions

If you are interested, read on. This next section gives you the scoop on how to host your own H20.

HOW TO HOST H20

1. Read through this introduction and get a feel for the concepts of H20. Watch all the DVDs. Begin to envision what could happen, what God could do through you.

2. Ask the Father for wisdom. Does He want you to do something like this? If so, ask for His guidance on whom to ask to join you in organizing the venture. Don't try to implement H20 alone.

3. Begin putting out feelers to those you think might want to be part of making H20 happen. Loan out some of the DVDs to friends. Get their reactions. Put together a small team of three or four people. It'll be fun.

4. Solidify your team. Here's what you'll need:

    a. Someone to offer a house or apartment as a meeting place

    b. Some who will make sure dinner is prepared each week

    c. Some to organize the Overnight Getaway

    d. Some to just be warm, supportive, prayerful partners

5. Get your team together about six weeks before you plan to begin and

    a. Pray together for God's power.

    b. Decide everyone's roles.

    c. Finalize the dates.

    d. Ask for God's guidance on whom to invite and for the boldness to actually follow through!

6. Begin inviting people to attend. The group should be at least half unchurched people. If your group is mostly believers, then the nonbelievers will feel intimidated and be less likely to discuss freely. They'll have a sense that the cards are stacked against them.

7. Touch base with your team members weekly. Encourage one another to continue inviting friends. Pray over the phone together.
8. Get together a week before your first session and
   a. Ask God for exactly what you are hoping for. Be specific.
   b. Go over everyone's roles.
   c. Encourage each other!
9. Begin! Hold the first session. Ask the team to arrive an hour early and pray together. Here's a typical timetable:
   7:00 Dinner
   7:45 DVD
   8:15 Discussion
   9:00 Close

Adjust this schedule to fit your needs.

10. The rest of the directions are detailed within each lesson.

Special Instructions for the DISCUSSION LEADER

This section contains tips for the person guiding the discussion. Memorize it! OK, you don't have to memorize it, but do read it, mull over it, make sure you digest the concepts. Then show these helps to another team member, and ask him or her to give you feedback after each discussion on how you are doing. (Scary, I know, but you can do it!)

Each chapter of this leader's guide contains a number of possible questions you could ask. However, you don't have to ask these exact questions. The guidebook includes more questions than you probably will have time to ask. So pick and choose the questions according to the group dynamics and amount of time you have. Also feel free to rephrase the questions to make them your own.

Here are some principles for leading a healthy discussion:

- **Pray!** Ask God to give you wisdom, a listening ear, a peace that passes understanding, and "a spirit of power, of love and of self-discipline" (2 Timothy 1:7).
- **Listen!** Hear what people are saying. Don't worry so much about what you are going to ask next that you miss what someone is saying now. Really listen, then respond out of what you hear.
- **Affirm all responses:** "Thank you, Ben." "That's very interesting, Elizabeth." No matter what participants say, do not criticize their remarks. What they just said might be antagonistic, foolish, or simply ridiculous, but do not directly disparage it. Instead, say something like, "That's interesting; what do the rest of you think?" Once you directly disapprove of someone's comments, then some people will never speak up again for fear of that disapproval. So let everyone share whatever he or she is thinking without criticism.
- **Affirm responses but do *not* endorse them** with comments such as "Now there's a great comment!" or "I couldn't agree with you more." Such endorsements tip your hand and leave others knowing their comments were not approved.
- **Don't give your opinion** about an issue unless it has already been fully discussed. Some people will see you as the leader, and once you speak, they will shut down. If someone asks for your opinion, you might say, "I'll be glad to give it, but let's hear from everyone else first."
- A real key is to *not* just ask one question right after another but to **follow up with what someone says.** This makes the discussion more like a conversation than a "lesson." Here are some good follow-up questions to have in your back pocket:
  - Can you give an example?
  - Explain what you mean.
  - When did you start thinking or feeling that way?

- How confident are you that it is true?
- How well does that work for you?
- That's interesting. What do the rest of you think?

Coach the other team members on how to help create a good atmosphere for open discussion. Here are some suggestions to pass on to them:

- **Be accepting of each person,** even when the person's behavior, speech, or lifestyle is dissimilar to yours. Shane Sooter, who directed the filming of H20, came to Christ through a program similar to this one. Some little old ladies invited him to a meal and video in one of their homes. He accepted, more for the home-cooked meal than anything else. He arrived with his ponytail, tattoos, and live-in girlfriend named Janna, who was pregnant. In Shane's words, "Though it must have been driving them crazy, those sweet ladies said nothing about our living situation. They simply loved and accepted us." By the end of the series, he and Janna had accepted Christ. At the appropriate time, the women pointed out that Jesus would want the couple to be married, and they were. Shane still has his ponytail and tattoos, but has made a significant life change. You can see Janna as the waitress in Episode 06. But Shane said if those ladies had criticized their lifestyle before they knew Christ, they would have been out of there. So overlook the coarse language and ignore the cigarette butts in your yard; don't comment about the alcohol on someone's breath. Remember, people who don't know Christ will act like they don't know Christ. Also remember, Jesus was known as a friend to sinners.

- Early on, if others aren't speaking up, jump in with your responses to help **"prime the pump."**

- **Try *not* to have your responses sound churchy or super-spiritual.** For example, when the question is asked, "Why did you decide to come to H20?" don't say, "Because I want to see others know Jesus and accept Him as Savior and be saved from Hell." While that answer may be true, it might be more prudent to say

"Tony told me about the study, and I am interested in spiritual things and wanted to be part of it. Plus I get a free meal every week!"

- **Do *not* be instructional,** trying to answer everyone's questions and solve everyone's problems. Once a know-it-all speaks up, the conversation shuts down.
- **Do give your opinion, but do it in a personal, humble way.** "My experience has been . . ." or "This is how I see it . . ."
- **Talk enough but not too much.** A little silence can be good for a group, so don't try to fill every quiet moment.
- **Try to listen** to the Spirit as well as to the conversation.
- **Pray silently** all through the DVD and discussion.

(Make copies of page 105 and give a copy to every team member.)

What do you do with the difficult, domineering, excessively talkative participant? Try these ideas:

1. If someone is talking on and on, interrupt . . . nicely. Say "I see what you mean. Let's see how others feel about that."
2. If someone is regularly talking too much, you might say "I'd like to give everyone a chance to say one thing before anyone speaks a second time."
3. If someone continues to dominate, step aside with him or her after a session. Say something like "I see you have a lot of ideas and are willing to express them. That's great. But I need your help. Some of the others aren't so bold. Would you help me draw them out? How?"
4. To a person(s) who never talks, you might say "Does anyone who hasn't spoken up yet have a thought?" If that doesn't work and the Spirit seems to be prompting you, you might say "Kevin, I noticed you haven't said anything. I'd be interested in hearing what you think."

> Above all, love each person in the group. If you truly care about them, they will sense it, and the Holy Spirit will flow through you!

Miscellaneous (yet important) tips for the LEADER

- Practice with your DVD player: make sure you know how to use it!
- Create a warm atmosphere in your home.
- Try to have dinner already prepared by the time people arrive so you aren't scrambling around.
- Dinner does not have to be fancy. Homey is better than fancy. If it is too fancy, people feel stiff and formal. Aim for comfortable and tasty!
- Set up the chairs for the DVD viewing in a way so everyone can see the TV. But for the discussion, you may want to rearrange the seating so it is a circle and everyone has a sense of being included.
- Once it's time for the DVD and discussion to start, turn the ringer off on your home phone to avoid an untimely interruption.
- You might have coffee available after the group ends. Those wanting to talk personally may be more likely to do so after the group breaks up.
- Let others help you clean up if they volunteer. It will make them feel more like they are part of what is going on, and it will help you get to bed earlier!

Helps for the OVERNIGHT GETAWAY COORDINATOR (pages 107 and 108)

The Overnight Getaway can be a powerful time of connection and decision. When people get away from the their usual haunts, they often can see life in a fresh way. Here are a few tips for the coordinator:

1. Find a suitable location.
   a. The best setting is someplace surrounded by nature so group members can take a walk or just drink in the beauty. God draws people to Him through His creation.
   b. Try Christian retreat centers, state park cabins, or rental condos. Maybe someone in the group or on the team has, or knows someone who has, a lake house or beach condo that would work.
   c. Keep the cost as low as possible for those who may not have a lot of extra money.
   d. Get accurate pricing to bring back to the group to avoid any surprises.
   e. Make sure your directions are clear and accurate. Give everyone the phone number of the place where you will be staying.
2. During the Overnight Getaway:
   a. Arrive early and make sure everything is as it should be.
   b. If the lodging does not have a TV and DVD player, arrange for them to be brought and set up. Be sure to try them out before the evening session begins.
   c. Take care of all the details as the home leader would: room setup, thermostat adjustment, prepare some snacks and drinks.
   d. Here's a sample Overnight Getaway timetable:

Friday

7:00 P.M.	Dinner
8:00 P.M.	View and discuss Episode 06.
9:15 P.M.	Snacks, hang out

Saturday

8:30 A.M. Breakfast

9:15 A.M. Encourage individuals to find a place alone and interact with the Reflection section from Episode 06.

10:30 A.M. View and discuss Episode 07.

Noon Lunch together

Afternoon Return home or plan something fun to do together.

For the WHOLE TEAM (page 109)

How do I invite someone?

Actually, asking people to come may be the most daunting part of this venture. But be encouraged. Once you get started, it gets easier. And usually you'll be surprised at who says yes. Here are a few keys:

- The most important thing you can do is to ask God to prepare the hearts of those you will invite.
- Most people do want connection and will be glad someone is interested in them.
- When inviting, avoid using the term *Christianity*. Instead, focus on Jesus. Rather than saying, "We're going to discuss what Christianity is all about," say, "We're going to look at who Jesus was and is."
- Do not trick people. Do not invite people for dinner, then spring the DVD on them. Be clear that you will watch and discuss a DVD about Jesus.
- To get you thinking, here are some suggestions on what you might say:
  - "Hey, there's a group of us getting together for dinner and to talk about spiritual things—would you be interested?"
  - "I'm going to a friend's house to watch a DVD talking about who Jesus really is. Would you consider going with me?"

- "Have you heard about H20? It's this really cool DVD that tells the truth about Jesus. We're going to discuss it over at _____'s house. We're also having dinner. I'd love for you to come."
- "I think you are probably going to Hell since you are not a Christian, but I know this home group that can show you the light. What'll it be: learn or burn?" (OK, probably better not to use this last one.)

- If they say they'll think about it, contact them again later just to say "I hope you'll come. I think you'll like it, but if you don't like it, you don't have to go back. What do you have to lose?"

FINAL QUIZ (page 110)

Jesus said in John 13:35, "By this all men will know that you are my disciples, if you . . ."

- a. know everything
- b. lead perfect lives
- c. win every argument
- d. have a clean house
- e. love each other

Besides inviting God's power into H20 through prayer, the most important factor in making this enterprise a success is actually caring about the people each of you invites. You can treat attenders in one of two ways: as projects or as people. This chart shows the difference:

PROJECTS	OR	PEOPLE
Someone to convince		Someone to care for
A goal, a target, an objective		A human, a name, an individual
A win/lose situation: either I win them to Christ or it was a waste		A win/win situation: even if they don't trust Jesus, I have shown them love and may have planted a seed for their future decision

The greatest commandment is not to win people to Christ but to love people regardless of how they respond to Christ. Paul made it clear that even if he were the greatest witness in the world but didn't have genuine love, his life would end up a big fat zero. So determine to love people. If you do that, no matter what else happens, you will have taken the most excellent way and become for someone else a taste of the living H20.

LEADER'S GUIDE

Thirsty

EPISODE 01

PURPOSE
- ❏ To help the group get comfortable with each other
- ❏ To set the mood and direction of the series
- ❏ To get everyone thinking about thirst—other people's and their own

PREPARATION
- ❏ Be sure to have dinner ready when folks arrive.
- ❏ Brew coffee for after dinner.
- ❏ Set out name tags.
- ❏ Have participants' guides ready to hand out.
- ❏ Cue DVD to Episode 01.
- ❏ Present a warm atmosphere with candles, soft music, or a fire in the fireplace.

PRAYER
Lord, please . . .
- ❏ influence those You are calling to actually come
- ❏ give those of us on the team warm, accepting, interested hearts
- ❏ open our eyes to Your truth
- ❏ steer the discussion toward honesty, openness, and truth

AT DINNER

Be ready with some conversation starters, in case the group is quiet.

- I would like everyone to meet my dog. Feed him at your own risk! Anyone else have a pet as intelligent as Fido Junior?
- Let's see who has the most interesting middle name! Mine is . . .
- Hey Aaron, where do you work?
    - How long have you been there?
    - What do you like about it?
- What's the best movie you've seen lately? How about the worst movie?

AFTER DINNER

Once you have gathered everyone to watch the DVD,

- Express your pleasure at everyone's presence.
- Explain that this is the first of ten gatherings. At each meeting there will be dinner, then a 20–30 minute presentation on DVD, followed by a discussion of about 30–40 minutes.
- The purpose of these get-togethers is to explore the person and message of Jesus.
- Next, hand out the participants' guides and ask everyone to turn to page 4.
- Read the opening "Welcome" paragraphs, and then read the ground rules.

   Welcome! We are glad you decided to take part in H2O. We don't think you'll regret it. Ever.

   The idea of these sessions is to explore Jesus, who He was and is, what He said, and what that means for you. There will be no heavy-handed preaching or manipulation. As a matter of fact, our group will abide by these principles:

Ground Rules

- **Everyone is free to express his or her views, whether he or she is in agreement with the DVD message or not.**
- **No one is allowed to criticize or attack someone else's view, although you may express your own when it disagrees with someone else's.**
- **No one has to talk at all. You can simply sit and listen, if you prefer.**
- **Conversely, no one is allowed to talk all the time.**
- **We will start the dinner at _____ o'clock and end each session by _____ o'clock.**

Pretty simple. Any questions?

LEADER'S NOTE: Boldface type will be used to signify what you as the leader might actually say. Please don't just read the content in boldface type, but rather put the content in your own words.

Regular type will indicate special instructions just for you.

Each gathering will include a meal, a half-hour DVD presentation, and then an open discussion. So, what's there to lose? Not much except some time out of your week. What is there to gain? At the least, a deeper understanding of what others believe and why. At the most, if what Jesus says is true, a way to quench the deepest thirst of your life.

Before we get started on tonight's DVD session, let's go around and introduce ourselves by telling one of your favorite places to go, one of your favorite things to do, and one of your favorite people to be with. If you don't want to answer, just say "Pass."

LEADER'S NOTE: You go first, modeling how you want the question answered. For instance, "My name is John Smith, and one of my favorite places to go is the mountains, and that's because one of my favorite things to do is snow ski. As for one of my favorite people, it's not actually a person, but my dog, whom you met earlier, Fido Junior."

If there is silence after only a couple of people share, say

Thanks. Now, as the ground rules stated, no one has to say anything, but before I move on, anyone else willing to share a favorite place, activity, and person?

Great! Well, it's good to get to know a little bit about each of you. Now let's watch the first session.

VIEW EPISODE 01 ▶ THIRSTY

DISCUSSION

LEADER'S NOTES:

- Remember, you can pick and choose questions based on
  - how the group discussion is progressing
  - how much time is left

- Try not to simply read the questions. Instead:
  - Ask follow-up questions based on what people say.
  - Put the questions in your own words.
  - Look up at the group when you ask them.
  - Use a conversational, interested tone.
- Questions with an * are suggested as particularly worthwhile.
- End on time!

*1. Kyle defined thirst as an inner desire that demands satisfaction and said that people are thirsty for something that can't be satisfied with the stuff of this world. What are your feelings about it?
  - If you feel people do experience that kind of deep thirst, how would you describe it?
  - If you don't think there is such a thirst, then how do you explain so many people feeling like there is?

*2. Oxford scholar C. S. Lewis was quoted in the presentation. His words are in your H20 participant's guide. Would someone be willing to read it?

> "Creatures are not born with desires unless satisfaction for those desires exists. A baby feels hunger: well, there is such a thing as food. A duckling wants to swim: well, there is such a thing as water. . . . If I find in myself a desire which no experience in this world can satisfy, the most probable explanation is that I was made for another world. If none of my earthly pleasures satisfy it, that does not prove that the universe is a fraud. Probably earthly pleasures were never meant to satisfy it, but only to arouse it, to suggest the real thing."
> —C. S. LEWIS, *MERE CHRISTIANITY*, p. 120, MacMillan, NY, 1979

Here are some other desires and their means of fulfillment:

Desire	Fulfillment
thirst	water
knowledge	information
companionship	people
children	procreation
accomplishment	success
recognition	awards
_____	_____
_____	_____

Can you think of others to add to the list?

Besides the deep-down thirst Kyle was talking about, can anyone think of a desire for which there is no fulfillment on earth?

3. We heard Kyle's story about buying a pillow off the Internet. Does anyone have a similar story?

Leader, if people do share their stories, ask—**What did you take away from the experience?**

4. Kyle suggested five ways we could view the possible fulfillment of our deepest thirst. As you approach this study, how would you describe your attitude? Again, don't feel you have to answer unless you really want to. These are listed in your participant's guide on page 6. Would you say you are more cynical, skeptical, curious, settled, or satisfied, and why do you say so?

- Cynical—certain that pretty much everything is a scam
- Skeptical—suspicious of everything (politicians, preachers, even your own brother!) and need clear proof before trusting anything
- Curious—interested in finding truth and open to whatever it may be

- Settled—fairly content but knowing that your deepest longings are not being met
- Satisfied—certain you have found what you are looking for and, as a result, thoroughly fulfilled

LEADER'S NOTE: Remember *not* to contradict a participant's answer. If a nonbeliever says "I'm really satisfied," do not reply with something like "You can't really be satisfied without Jesus" or "You must be fooling yourself!" However, you might ask something like "Do you think there is any possibility that you are sitting by the hotel pool and missing the ocean?" If the nonbeliever still says he is completely satisfied, just say in a nonjudgmental tone, "OK, thanks. Anyone else?"

5. If you were uncertain how to answer the question or if you want to be sure your response is accurate, here is one way to clear it up. Do you really believe Mandi lost her wedding ring in the ocean, and then Vince and Kyle found it later with an underwater metal detector in near total darkness? Silently choose from one of these options:

- "No way! That has to be bogus."
- "It's doubtful. I'd have to see some convincing proof."
- "It's possible. I'd be interested in hearing more about it."
- "Who cares? What does it matter?"
- "I'm not sure, but I do know I've had equally thrilling experiences in my life."

If you said . . .

- "No way! What a fake," then you are probably a cynic.
- "It's doubtful. I'd have to see more proof," then you are probably a skeptic.
- "That's interesting. I'd like to hear more about it," then you are probably curious.
- "Who cares? What does it matter?" then you are probably someone who settles for what you have and doesn't look for more.

- "I'm not sure its true, but I've had thrilling things happen in my life," then you are most likely learning to be satisfied.

6. Do you find this little assessment to be an accurate gauge of your attitude toward new information in life?

*7. What do you think is the likelihood that Jesus can fill a person's deepest thirst? What makes you think so?

WRAP UP

This has been a great night! I really appreciate everyone being here. A couple of things I found very interesting were . . .

LEADER: Sum up some of the key insights of the evening as you saw them.

Before we close, I'd just like to point out the "For Reflection" section of your H20 participant's guide. Notice that you don't have to mull over these questions—it is totally optional. But it might be helpful in thinking through our topics, so I hope you will at least try it.

Now I'd like to end our evening with a prayer, but feel free to hang around as long as you like. There's more coffee and dessert for anyone who would like some.

LEADER: Pray a very short and simple prayer. Avoid long, churchy prayers that might seem showy, be intimidating, or just turn off nonbelievers. You might try something like the following:

> *Lord, I am glad to be here with these folks tonight. Show us how we can find satisfaction for the deepest thirsts within us. This week, would you watch over and protect each person in this group? Amen.*

LEADER'S NOTE:
- If you think it would be appropriate, send a card or e-mail to those who attended just to say how glad you are that they came.

- Call those who didn't show up (or have the person who invited them call) just to say you missed them.

⏪ FOR REFLECTION

These are optional thought questions to ponder or respond to in writing between sessions. You will *not* be asked to share them in the next session, but you may find it helpful to talk them over with a friend.

Is there anything you picked up from the DVD or group time that you would like to think more about or be sure to remember?

Try to describe your own deep thirst, if you feel you have one.

Do you experience this thirst at certain times more than others? If so, when are those times of intensified thirst?

Why might you feel this thirst more at these times?

What have you found to be the thirst-quenching ability of . . .

Money	Zero	Low	Medium	High	Complete
Possessions	Zero	Low	Medium	High	Complete
Success	Zero	Low	Medium	High	Complete
Relationships	Zero	Low	Medium	High	Complete

When you do get thirsty in the deeper sense, what do you generally turn to in order to quench your thirst?

Describe how well it works.

> *Jesus stood and said in a loud voice,*
> *"If anyone is thirsty,*
> *let him come to me and drink."*
> —JOHN 7:37

LEADER'S GUIDE

Polluted

EPISODE 02

PURPOSE
- ❏ To honestly acknowledge, and apologize for, the failures of the church and its people
- ❏ To help participants separate Jesus and who He is from the church and what it is like

PREPARATION
- ❏ Be sure to have dinner ready before participants arrive.
- ❏ Set out name tags.
- ❏ Cue DVD to Episode 02.
- ❏ Present a warm atmosphere with music, candles, etc.
- ❏ * Be ready with some details on the overnighter to present to the group.

PRAYER
Lord, please . . .
- ❏ influence those invited, to return
- ❏ help the believers present avoid defensiveness when negative comments are made about the church, Christians, or even You
- ❏ guide the discussion toward honesty, openness, and truth

* designates a new preparation item

SPECIAL LEADER'S NOTE: In this episode, we want to allow participants to express their views, both negative and positive, regarding the church and Christians. As members of Christ's body on earth, we want to admit that in countless ways Christ's followers have poorly imitated Him. As participants express negative or derogatory things about the church and Christians, do not try to defend, excuse, or explain. Simply listen, and mourn with those who have been hurt by the poor replicas of Jesus in this world (including us!).

Be sure to encourage the other believers in your group to resist the urge to become defensive as well.

AT DINNER

In case the group is still reserved, be ready with some conversation starters. These are just examples; come up with your own if you wish:

- I don't know if I've heard where everyone grew up. I grew up [tell about yourself]. **How about you, Josh?**
- What is the most trouble you ever got into at school?
- Anybody have any fun this week? What did you do?
- Last week you met my dog, and I told you how intelligent he is. Well, this week let me introduce you to an even more intelligent pet—my goldfish named Sharkbait!

AFTER DINNER

Once you have gathered everyone to watch the DVD . . .

- I'd just like to say again that it is great to have you all back this week. I am especially glad that none of you died as a result of my cooking!
- Before we play tonight's DVD, I have a question. What's the nastiest thing you have ever eaten or drunk?

VIEW EPISODE 02 ▶ POLLUTED

DISCUSSION

LEADER'S NOTES:

- Remember, you can pick and choose from these questions.
- Questions with an * are suggested as particularly worthwhile.
- Do not be defensive! Just let people speak their experience with no judgment whatsoever.
- Even better, affirm each answer with a nod or "uh-huh."
- Be sure to end on time!

  *1. Kyle used words like *boring, outdated,* and *hypocritical* to describe a lot of people's experience of church. What words would you use to describe your experience of church? Just say them out loud as they come to you.

  - Anyone else?

2. How about when I say the word *Christians?* What comes to mind then?

*3. Kyle thinks that Christians often give the impression that Jesus is someone who hates rock and roll, never smiles, and wears His tie too tight. If you had to describe Jesus *from your church experience alone,* what would you say He is like?

   - How close do you think this church view of Jesus is to the real Jesus?

*4. When Kyle went door to door asking people why they didn't attend church, he found that most people didn't say things like "I don't believe in God" or "I think the Bible is a bunch of fairy tales." Instead, he heard things like "Church is boring" or "I don't understand what the preacher is talking about" or "I'm busy." When it comes to faith, would you say your primary problem is with Jesus and what He is like or with the church and what it is like? Before you answer, I realize it could be with both, but if it is both, with which do you have a bigger struggle—Jesus or the church? If you want to explain, fine, but don't feel like you have to.

*5. One of the perversions of Christianity is turning it into a bunch of rules. When Kyle was talking about this, he listed some old laws that were pretty funny. Look in your H2O participant's guide at page 9. Let's take a vote! Which of these laws do you think should still be on the books?

For	Against	
_____	_____	A person may not wear cowboy boots unless he owns at least three cows.
_____	_____	Owners of homes with Christmas lights up past February 2nd will be fined $250.
_____	_____	Gathering and consuming roadkill shall be illegal.
_____	_____	No more than five inoperable vehicles may occupy one piece of property at one time.
_____	_____	A woman may not buy a hat without her husband's permission.
_____	_____	Women should not be allowed to drive a motorized vehicle unless a man precedes it waving a red flag to warn oncoming pedestrians or motorists.

6. Sometimes critics of faith will cite ancient Jewish laws to prove that Christianity is ridiculous and outdated. Here are some unusual laws from the Old Testament. As I read each one, say if you would vote for or against this law today.

For	Against	
_____	_____	Do not cook a young goat in the milk from its mother (Exodus 23:19).
_____	_____	Do not tattoo your body (Leviticus 19:28).
_____	_____	Do not clip off the edges of your beard (Leviticus 19:27).
_____	_____	No work is to be done on the Sabbath, i.e., Saturday (Exodus 20:10).
_____	_____	Attach tassels to the corners of your garments (Numbers 15:38).
_____	_____	Do not eat anything that has been killed by a wild animal (*Jewish equivalent of Tennessee's law against eating road kill?* Exodus 22:31).
_____	_____	Do not eat camel, rabbit, or eel, no matter how it is killed (Leviticus 11:4–10).

7. Laws like the ones I've just read made good sense at the time they were instituted, though now we may be unsure of the reason. For instance, in the Old Testament, tattoos were forbidden because of their association with the worship of false gods. Actually, we all formulate some pretty specific rules to live by. For example,

   - What kinds of rules do parents have for their kids?
   - How about coaches making rules for their players?
   - Would you say that everyone makes up rules for his or her life, like "I'll make the most of my life" or "I'll treat others with tolerance" or "I'll keep in shape"?
   - Would you say that most people also transfer their rules to others: "Everyone should make the most of his or her life; everyone should treat others with tolerance; everyone should keep in shape"?

8. **Why do we make up rules? I mean, what do they do for us?**

Possible answers might include:

- Rules tell us exactly what to do; they give us direction.
- Rules tell us when we are doing well and when we aren't.
- Rules can be used to control and judge other people.

9. **What are the limitations or weaknesses of living by a set of do's and do not's?**

Possible answers might include:

- Rules tend to be inflexible.
- Rules can become outdated.
- Rules can't meet every situation.
- Rules multiply until they become overwhelming.
- Rules can cause us to take our focus off the higher principles like love, justice, and kindness.

*10. **There are a lot of do's and do not's in the Bible, and that is why a lot of people think being a Christian is all about following rules. But the Bible says that one reason God gave all these rules was to make it clear that people cannot follow all the rules—that perfect rule-based living is impossible. Look in your H2O guidebooks at page 9. Follow along as I read these two passages from the Bible.**

> *"Now do you see it? No one can ever be made right in God's sight by doing what the law commands. For the more we know of God's laws, the clearer it becomes that we aren't obeying them."* —ROMANS 3:20, *LB*

> *So what was the law for? It was given to show that the wrong things people do are against God's will. . . . In other words, the law was our guardian leading us to Christ.* —GALATIANS 3:19, 24, *NCV*

So despite what you might have been told, Christianity is NOT about rule-following. Would you agree that following all the right rules and doing everything perfectly is impossible? Why or why not?

*11. **Besides rule-based living, Kyle mentioned other distortions of Jesus' message.**

- He talked about what one writer termed "Christianity and . . ."; that is, stuff added to Jesus like political and social agendas, or even personal opinions. He said such additions are like nasty ranchero sauce added to a good burrito. What have you seen added to the basic message of Jesus?
- Kyle also mentioned that Christians can be weird, not just different in a good way but really truly bizarre. I would ask if you know any weird Christians, but I'm afraid my name might come up, so let's move on!
- Then churches have sometimes been like the one-hour cleaners, making claims that they don't back up. Anyone want to add to this list?

*12. In the DVD, the minister reads Luke 15:1, 2 from the Bible:

Now the tax collectors and "sinners" were all gathering around to hear him. But the Pharisees and the teachers of the law muttered, "This man welcomes sinners and eats with them."

- The religious leaders of His day saw Jesus as a person who readily connected with those whom others viewed as immoral. How close is this description to your view of Jesus? Would you say pretty close? Or quite distant? Why?
- In what way is your view different from this one?

*13. Are you willing to consider Jesus on His own terms, apart from how today's church might represent Him?

WRAP UP

I have enjoyed and appreciated the discussion tonight.

- Don't forget the "For Reflection" section of your participant's guide, for those of you who are interested.
- Also, this may sound like a wacky idea, but I'd like us to consider all of us taking an overnight getaway together. We have a great place to go. We could meet there on a Friday night, have dinner, and watch and discuss one of the DVDs; then the next day watch another DVD and discuss it, and then maybe have some fun. Just think about it. It's not final. But we can talk more about it next week.

- **And please remember to bring your participant's guide next week because we will use it during the discussion. Great to have you all.**
- **Let me close in prayer.**

Again, just a brief non-churchy prayer of thanks to God, asking His blessing on the group. Here's an example:

> *Lord, thanks again for this group and this study. I ask you to be with each person in our group and help each one with whatever he or she may need. Amen.*

◄◄ FOR REFLECTION

These are optional thought questions to ponder or respond to in writing between sessions. You will *not* be asked to share them in the next session but may find it helpful to talk them over with a friend.

Of the pollutants Kyle mentioned, which has particularly bothered you?

- the boring, monotonous nature of so many churches
- making following Jesus all about keeping certain rules
- political or social agendas, and personal opinions added onto Jesus' message
- the hypocrisy of those who claim to be following Him
- the general weirdness of Christians
- something else: _____

If you had an important message to tell the world but other people came along and twisted, polluted, and added to it, how would you feel?

What would you imagine to be Jesus' reaction to the abuses and misuses of His message?

The Bible actually tells us not to blindly trust people, *especially* those who claim to be communicating messages from God. That's because people will let us down. People will intentionally mislead. People are polluted. John, one of Jesus' closest followers, wrote,

> *My dear friends, don't believe everything you hear.*
> *Carefully weigh and examine what people tell you.*
> *Not everyone who talks about God comes from God.*
> *There are a lot of lying preachers loose in the world.*
> —1 JOHN 4:1, *THE MESSAGE*

Try writing out your view of Jesus; that is, try to describe Him as you see Him.

> **Where did you get your information for what you just wrote? Check all that apply.**
>
> ____ from accounts of Him recorded in the Bible
>
> ____ from what I've read in books or magazines
>
> ____ from how the church represents Him
>
> ____ from the way Christians act
>
> ____ from the attitudes of my parents, professors, friends, etc.
>
> - Which aspects of your view came from eyewitness descriptions of Him like those found in the Bible? Circle them.
> - Which came from less-than-reliable sources? Cross them out.
> - Which came from . . . well, you don't know where? Put a question mark beside those.

The preacher in the DVD described Jesus this way:

> The love of Jesus is not conditional.
> It isn't based on ulterior motives.
> It has no hidden agendas.
> There's nothing you can do to deserve it.
> And there's nothing you can do to lose it.
> It's free. It's powerful. It's pure.

Are you willing to consider Jesus on His own terms, to see if He is like what this preacher described?

Remember to bring this participant's guide to the next gathering.

> *"Never will I leave you;
> never will I forsake you."*
> —HEBREWS 13:5

Source

PURPOSE
- ❏ To introduce and discuss the concept of God as a loving Father

PREPARATION
- ❏ * Have pens available for everyone.
- ❏ * Have a few copies of the pages needed out of the participant's guide for those who forget their books.
- ❏ * Call those who missed last week to say you missed them.
- ❏ Have dinner ready before participants arrive.
- ❏ Set out name tags.
- ❏ Cue DVD to Episode 03.
- ❏ Present a warm atmosphere with music, candles, etc.

PRAYER
Lord, please . . .
- ❏ prepare the participants' hearts to see You as the loving, gracious, forgiving Father that You are
- ❏ prod those who didn't come last week to return this week

* designates new preparation items

AT DINNER

By now the group should be talking without the need for you to begin conversation. Just in case, think in advance of some topics you might discuss during dinner: the latest book someone has read, a big sports event, their all-time worst teacher in school.

AFTER DINNER

Once you have gathered everyone to watch the DVD, say

> Great to have you back. Tonight we start with a multiple-choice question. What do you think is the most common descriptive term for God in the New Testament section of the Bible? Here are your choices:
>
> King   Father   Almighty   Judge   Holy One

39

Thanks for your responses. We'll hear the correct answer in this DVD session, so let's crank it up!

VIEW EPISODE 03 ▶ SOURCE

DISCUSSION

1. If you are willing to say, who did you find yourself identifying with, or resonating with, most: the Korean-American girl, her mother, Kyle's daughter, or Kyle as the good dad?

*2. What is your reaction to the fact that the most common descriptive name for God in the New Testament is "Father"?

*3. Most people believe in some sort of a higher power. What is your view of God? How would you describe Him?

*4. Turn to page 13 in your participant's guide. Here are some descriptive words for God based on the Bible.

   ✓ Check those you believe are absolutely true of God.

   X Mark an X beside those you believe are NOT true of God.

   ? Place a question mark beside those about which you just aren't sure.

___ living (alive)	___ infinite (no beginning or end)	___ eternal
___ omnipotent (all-powerful)	___ omniscient (all-knowing)	___ omnipresent (present everywhere)
___ holy (perfect)	___ wise	___ impartial
___ loving	___ patient	___ compassionate
___ forgiving	___ faithful	___ generous
___ kind	___ responsive	___ personal

Count up your check marks in the shaded section and count up your check marks in the unshaded section. Notice which has more.

> The shaded section contains characteristics of God that are more impersonal, distant, and non-relational. The unshaded section contains descriptive words that are more personal, intimate, and relational. My theory is that most people will have more check marks in the shaded area. Does your count support my theory or go against it?

If their answers seem to support the theory, ask, **Any reason why, do you think?**

5. One inaccurate view of God is that of an angry father. You may wonder why negative words such as angry are not on this list describing God. While anger may be a temporary reaction to evil, a reaction that flows out of God's holiness, anger is not an ongoing characteristic of God as He is in and of himself. Look at the Scripture on page 14 in your participant's guide.

> *His anger lasts only a moment,*
> *but his favor lasts a lifetime.*
> —PSALM 30:5

> A good parent might sometimes get angry, but anger is not who he or she is. That's how the Bible describes God: He may get angry, but He is not angry in the same way He is loving or kind. Do you think this distinction between what God sometimes does and what He is in and of himself is valid? Why or why not?

*6. Psychologists say that our primary view of God usually comes from our interaction with our earthly dads. Let's do one other experiment tonight to see if that is true of this group. On page 14 of your participant's guide, mark a *D* at the place on each line that depicts how you experienced your dad when you were little, say, in elementary school. If you didn't have a dad, choose the closest thing to a father figure you had.

Give your own example:

> When I was little, my dad was pretty busy and stern. He changed later, but when I was a kid, that's what he was like. So I would put my *D* about three-fourths of the way down toward the right end of that line.

Hold the book up to show what you mean.

Any questions?

Gentle ----------------------------------G----------D---------- Stern
Close--- Distant
Talkative--- Silent
Patient-- Explosive
Joyful-- Somber
Encouraging--Critical
Interested--- Apathetic
Kind--- Harsh
Honest--- Deceitful
Consistent--- Erratic

> **Now go back and put a *G* on each line at the place that represents how you see God these days. For example, I probably see God as more stern than gentle, so I would put my *G* a little over halfway to the right. OK? Questions?**
>
> **How is your experience of your dad when you were a kid similar to how you see God now? What does this little exercise show you?**

*7. Would you welcome or resist the concept of a loving heavenly Father? Why?

8. What would be some general common objections to believing in a loving, fatherly God?

LEADER: The question of pain and suffering is bound to come up at this point—"I can't believe in a loving God with so much hurt in the world." You have two choices.

1. You can simply refer people to the accompanying resource called *Storm*, which speaks to this question, as well as many others. Read to the group the topics it covers. Offer to loan it out to anyone interested. It's best if you have watched *Storm* in advance and can recommend it.

2. Use the helps below in the boxed section to briefly discuss suffering, and then recommend *Storm*.

> **The question of suffering is a big one. Why do you think there is so much suffering in the world?**
>
> **Are suffering and a loving God incompatible?**
>
> **Can you think of any reason why God would allow so much hurt?**
>
> **LEADER:** After the discussion on suffering, you might summarize it. Affirm that though we can't explain all suffering, there are some good reasons why bad things happen, and suffering does not disprove the existence of a loving God. You may also add . . .
>
> **We can't give a full answer to the question of suffering in this session. But here are two considerations that show it is possible for God to be both loving and allow pain.**
>
> 1. **Good people cause suffering. Surgeons cut people open; coaches make players run sprints; friends give each other feedback they don't want to hear.**
> 2. **Good people sometimes allow others to go through pain in order to preserve the other person's self-determination or free will.**
>
> **For example:**
>
> **A father may let his daughter enter a marriage he knows will be difficult rather than try to control her.**
>
> **A mother may not oppose her son entering the military though she knows it will mean hardship, discipline, and possibly death.**
>
> **Loving people allow pain all the time. So it could be God views preserving our free will as worth all the hardship free will causes.**
>
> **You may not agree that God is loving, but does everyone agree that a loving being could possibly be in charge of a world that includes great suffering?**

*9. What impact would it make on your life if you did see God as a patient, loving, forgiving Father?

WRAP UP

Well, it's time to wrap up. This has been a very interesting discussion.

- Let me recommend again the "For Reflection" section of your participant's guide. By the way, has anyone taken a shot at doing these, and if so, any reaction? Great! Thank you for the feedback.
- Let's also talk about our reactions to the Overnight Getaway idea. What we would do is not meet the week before because we will watch a couple of the DVDs there. _____ can tell us more about it. She's been scouting places, just in case we decide to do it.

Openly discuss the idea. Let the group decide.

- And again, stay as long as you would like tonight.
- Let me close with a prayer.

> *Father—I call You that because that is what the Bible calls You—would You teach us what it means to say that You are our Father? Thank You. Amen.*

◄ FOR REFLECTION

During the group discussion, you were asked to mark which of the characteristics of God seem true to you, which seem false, and which you were unsure of. Look at them again, but this time think of them in terms of which ones you *experience* as you relate to God. For instance, you may think that God is kind, but you may not experience this kindness when you try to relate to Him.

E   Place an *E* beside those you experience personally.

B   Place a *B* beside those you believe but do *not* experience.

___ Leave the others blank.

___ living (alive)	___ infinite (no beginning or end)	___ eternal
___ omnipotent (all-powerful)	___ omniscient (all-knowing)	___ omnipresent (present everywhere)
___ holy (perfect)	___ wise	___ impartial

___ loving   ___ patient   ___ compassionate

___ forgiving   ___ faithful   ___ generous

___ kind   ___ responsive   ___ personal

What did this exercise reveal to you, if anything?

The lyrics of the song "Beautiful Like This," by Josh Wilson, were played during the DVD presentation. See if you relate.

> The fading sun and rising moon
> Are fighting for the afternoon
> The day gives in and yields its light
> The stars wake up to keep the night
> As your glory fills the sky I wonder
> How could you consider me
> So much more than all I see
> Because I am not, have never been
> Beautiful like this

My weary words and broken lives
Are set beneath your summer skies
What's worn and wrong, what's good and right
Are laid before my eyes tonight
As your glory fills the sky I wonder
How could you consider me
So much more than all I see
Because I am not, and never been
Beautiful like this

But you make all things new
Yes, you make all things new
I'm beautiful in you
That's how you could consider me
So much more than all I see
Redemption calls to broken men,
It heals their wounds, removes their sin

Your purest love was humbly spent
To bind my heart, and draw me in
Where I become whole again
I'm beautiful like this

Here are some reasons a person may resist the idea of God being a loving Father. If you find yourself pushing away any thought of a loving heavenly Father, do any of these lie beneath that resistance?

____ I just don't believe it's possible that God is like that.

____ I feel so unworthy of that kind of love.

____ I used to believe it, but too many bad things have happened to me.

____ I've been burned too many times when I've trusted someone to be loving.

____ I don't want to believe in a God of any kind because that would mean I would have to do things His way.

___ I am uncomfortable with the experience or feeling of love. It's just too . . . squishy!

___ Other _____

You might want to slowly make your way through these Scriptures that highlight God as Father. Underline anything that stands out to you.

A father to the fatherless, a defender of widows,
is God in his holy dwelling. —PSALM 68:5

"Which of you, if his son asks for bread, will give him a stone?
Or if he asks for a fish, will give him a snake?
If you, then, though you are evil, know how to give good gifts to your children,
how much more will your Father in heaven give good gifts to those who ask him! —MATTHEW 7:9–11

One day Jesus was praying in a certain place.
When he finished, one of his disciples said to him,
"Lord, teach us to pray, just as John taught his disciples."
He said to them, "When you pray, say:
"'Father, . . .'" —LUKE 11:1, 2

For you did not receive a spirit that makes you a slave again to fear,
but you received the Spirit of sonship. And by him we cry, "Abba, Father."
The Spirit himself testifies with our spirit that we are God's children.
—ROMANS 8:15, 16 (*Abba* is Aramaic for Daddy)

Give praise to the God and Father of our Lord Jesus Christ!
He is the Father who gives tender love.
All comfort comes from him. —2 CORINTHIANS 1:3, 4, *NIRV*

"I will be a Father to you,
and you will be my sons and daughters,
says the Lord Almighty." —2 CORINTHIANS 6:18

You have forgotten that word of hope.
It speaks to you as children. It says,
"My son, think of the Lord's training as important.
Do not lose hope when he corrects you.
The Lord trains those he loves.
He punishes everyone he accepts as a son." —HEBREWS 12:5, 6, *NIRV*

> *How great is the love the Father has lavished on us,*
> *that we should be called children of God!*
> *And that is what we are!* —1 JOHN 3:1

Could you talk to a fatherly God like these passages describe? If you are willing, try it.

LEADER'S GUIDE

EPISODE 04

PURPOSE
- ❏ To introduce Jesus as the one who has the ability to quench our deepest thirst

PREPARATION
- ❏ Call any who missed last week.
- ❏ Have dinner ready.
- ❏ Set out name tags.
- ❏ Cue DVD to Episode 04.
- ❏ Present a warm atmosphere with music, candles, etc.
- ❏ *Ask a believer in the group to be ready to close in prayer. Remind him or her that all you want is a brief, simple prayer, with no churchy language.

PRAYER
Lord, please . . .
- ❏ give participants the desire and energy to return
- ❏ provide us all with humility to admit our real thirsts
- ❏ open blind eyes to see Jesus as the ultimate thirst-quencher

* designates new preparation items

AFTER DINNER

Once you have gathered everyone to watch the DVD, ask:

Are there any foods you didn't like as a child but now do? If so, what?

Are there any foods you used to like but don't now that you've eaten my cooking? OK, just kidding. Let's watch the next session!

VIEW EPISODE 04 ▶ PURE

DISCUSSION

1. **How did you find yourself relating to the woman in the story? I mean, did you find yourself liking her, disliking her, connecting with her, criticizing her?**

2. What do you think she was thirsting for in her life?

*3. This may be a dangerous question to ask, but in your experience can relationships with other people fulfill the deepest thirsts in our lives?

4. If Jesus is exactly the way He was portrayed in this story, how would you feel toward Him? Would you be attracted? turned off?

*5. Look in your participant's guide on page 19. Jesus said He came to
- proclaim good news to the poor
- announce freedom for prisoners
- bring recovery of sight to the blind
- release the oppressed

This claim is recorded in Luke 4. The claim is fleshed out a bit in the boxed section. As I read what's there, see which needs you can relate to personally.

- Poor: feeling destitute materially, emotionally, relationally, or spiritually
- Captive: boxed in or controlled by others such as your parents, your past, your work situation, or just society in general
- Blind: unable to see clearly, make sense of it all, or figure out how to make life work
- Oppressed: dominated or tormented by inner demons, addictions, anger, or forces that seem to be more powerful than you

You won't have to answer this question, but which need do you connect with most?

LEADER'S NOTE: Usually, participants should answer first, but this is a good time for you to go first, exhibiting an appropriate level of vulnerability. For example:

For me, I sometimes feel oppressed, like the whole world is weighing down on me. I get discouraged, I want to quit, I eat too much. I would love to just be free of that sense of unlimited duty and expectation I so often feel.

*6. In your participant's guide is a list of options. Which do you sense is most likely to provide you the freedom or power you are looking for to satisfy your deepest needs? And why do you think so?

[ ] Rules: a solid system of do's and do not's

[ ] Stuff: a lot of inanimate material possessions

[ ] People: relationships with other human beings

[ ] God: a relationship with a divine being

[ ] Self: something within, yet untapped

[ ] Combination: a mixture of some or all of the above

7. Psychologists say people often don't find the help they need because they hide. They know they have ugly stuff inside that will turn others off, so they fake what they are like.

    a. If this is so, what percentage of others' real selves would you say we see?

    b. What keeps us from letting others see everything about us?

    c. Would you want to be around someone who knew absolutely everything about you?

    d. What do you think would happen if those closest to you suddenly knew everything about you?

    e. Would anyone here say you are fully honest with another human about everything—and I mean everything—in your life? If so, what's that like for you?

8. If you had a really close friend and then found out he or she had a serious flaw—was hooked on crack or had been arrested for armed robbery or had a porn problem—what would you do? How would you relate to that friend?

    What would that response say about you, about what you are like?

*9. Kyle claimed that Jesus knows everything about you, yet still loves you. "The one who knows you the best loves you the most." Do you think this is possible? If not, what makes it hard to believe?

*10. Kyle tells his story of guacamole. By the way, do you think Kyle is obsessed with food? Two weeks ago, ranchero sauce, this week guacamole—and both having to do with burritos! Very interesting. Some of us told our own stories of foods we used to despise but now enjoy. What's the possibility that you have been disliking Jesus, when in reality, if you really knew Him, you would enjoy what He offers?

*11. Some religious leaders say, "I will show you the way to truth so you can have real life." Jesus says, "I am the way and the truth and the life" (John 14:6). In another place, He said, "I am the bread of life. He who comes to me will never go hungry, and he who believes in me will never be thirsty" (John 6:35). What do you think of this claim?

*12. Complete this sentence: "I believe Jesus (can/cannot/might be able to) quench my thirst because . . ."

WRAP UP

Another great night of discussion. It's time to wrap up.

- You can find the Bible passage portrayed in the DVD in the "For Reflections" section of your participant's guide on pages 20–22. It's well worth reading.

- Also, if hearing this story of Jesus sparked your interest—or you just aren't sure what to make of Him—rather than taking our word for what He's like, let me challenge you to read one of the accounts of His life found in the Bible books of Matthew, Mark, Luke, or John.

- Lastly, I'm looking forward to being with you all at the overnight getaway. It will be great. I think you'll be glad you came.

- I've asked _____ to end our time with a prayer.

◄◄ FOR REFLECTION

Which of these statements rings true to you?

- ❑ Jesus can't help me.
- ❑ Jesus wants nothing to do with me.
- ❑ Jesus is making an offer too good to be true.
- ❑ Jesus is more interested in me being good than in me myself.
- ❑ Jesus is interested in me even though He knows all about me.

Try reading the whole story of Jesus and the woman of Samaria as told in John 4. As you do, underline anything that stands out or that you have questions about.

> *Now he had to go through Samaria. So he came to a town in Samaria called Sychar, near the plot of ground Jacob had given to his son Joseph. Jacob's well was there, and Jesus, tired as he was from the journey, sat down by the well. It was about the sixth hour.*
>
> *When a Samaritan woman came to draw water, Jesus said to her, "Will you give me a drink?" (His disciples had gone into the town to buy food.) The Samaritan woman said to him, "You are a Jew and I am a Samaritan woman. How can you ask me for a drink?" (For Jews do not associate with Samaritans.)*
>
> *Jesus answered her, "If you knew the gift of God and who it is that asks you for a drink, you would have asked him and he would have given you living water."*
>
> *"Sir," the woman said, "you have nothing to draw with and the well is deep. Where can you get this living water? Are you greater than our father Jacob, who gave us the well and drank from it himself, as did also his sons and his flocks and herds?"*
>
> *Jesus answered, "Everyone who drinks this water will be thirsty again, but whoever drinks the water I give him will never thirst. Indeed, the water I give him will become in him a spring of water welling up to eternal life."*
>
> *The woman said to him, "Sir, give me this water so that I won't get thirsty and have to keep coming here to draw water."*

He told her, "Go, call your husband and come back."

"I have no husband," she replied.

Jesus said to her, "You are right when you say you have no husband. The fact is, you have had five husbands, and the man you now have is not your husband. What you have just said is quite true."

"Sir," the woman said, "I can see that you are a prophet. Our fathers worshiped on this mountain, but you Jews claim that the place where we must worship is in Jerusalem."

Jesus declared, "Believe me, woman, a time is coming when you will worship the Father neither on this mountain nor in Jerusalem. You Samaritans worship what you do not know; we worship what we do know, for salvation is from the Jews. Yet a time is coming and has now come when the true worshipers will worship the Father in spirit and truth, for they are the kind of worshipers the Father seeks. God is spirit, and his worshipers must worship in spirit and in truth."

The woman said, "I know that Messiah (called Christ) is coming." "When he comes, he will explain everything to us."

Then Jesus declared, "I who speak to you am he."

Just then his disciples returned and were surprised to find him talking with a woman. But no one asked, "What do you want?" or "Why are you talking with her?"

Then, leaving her water jar, the woman went back to the town and said to the people, "Come, see a man who told me everything I ever did. Could this be the Christ?" They came out of the town and made their way toward him.

. . . . .

Many of the Samaritans from that town believed in him because of the woman's testimony, "He told me everything I ever did." So when the Samaritans came to him, they urged him to stay with them, and he stayed two days. And because of his words many more became believers.

They said to the woman, "We no longer believe just because of what you said; now we have heard for ourselves, and we know that this man really is the Savior of the world." —JOHN 4:4–30, 39–42

Based on what you just read, would Jesus be the kind of person you would like to know? Why or why not?

[ ] Yes!   [ ] No!   [ ] Maybe

_____

_____

_____

> If you would like to know more about Jesus, try reading one of the accounts of His life found in the Bible books of Matthew, Mark, Luke, or John. Start with any of them; they are all good! Use a modern translation that's understandable. If you have a Bible that is difficult to understand, buy a more up-to-date version. Your H2O leader can probably help you choose a good translation.
>
> Oftentimes, writing our thoughts helps us clarify our thinking. Now that you have had four weeks of study, what thoughts or questions do you have about Jesus?

*I am the way
and the truth
and the life.*
—JESUS, JOHN 14:6

 LEADER'S GUIDE

Mirage

 EPISODE 05

PURPOSE
- ❏ To consider whether or not the world can satisfy our thirsts

PREPARATION
- ❏ Have dinner ready.
- ❏ Set out name tags if needed.
- ❏ Cue DVD to Episode 05.
- ❏ Present a warm atmosphere.

PRAYER
Lord, please . . .
- ❏ give us all the honesty and strength to evaluate how well our usual thirst-quenching methods work
- ❏ help us to know Jesus as the one who can satisfy our needs for purpose, security, and love

AFTER DINNER

Once you have gathered everyone to watch the DVD, ask:

> Does anyone have any unusual names in your family history? For instance, I had a grandfather named Fletcher and a great-grandfather named Bismarck—not real common.
>
> Can anyone recall the first AND last names of your great-grandparents? Can you tell us anything else about them? How about your great-great-grandparents?
>
> OK, let's watch the next episode!

VIEW EPISODE 05 ▶ MIRAGE

DISCUSSION

*1. Have you ever believed that a certain thing—a car, job, or person—would fulfill you if only you could get it? If you did get it, what was it like?

- Was it everything you imagined it would be?

*2. Do you believe that if, like Solomon, you had just about everything you wanted that you too would end up saying "Meaningless! Meaningless!" (Ecclesiastes 1:2)? Why or why not?

*3. In your experience, what can possessions do for you, and what can't they do for you?

LEADER'S NOTE: Here are some possible answers:

- CAN provide comfort, status, respect, impress people
- CANNOT guarantee good health, buy love, protect from death

4. Solomon wrote, "Whoever loves money never has money enough; whoever loves wealth is never satisfied with his income" (Ecclesiastes 5:10). Would you agree or disagree?

*5. In your experience, what can achievement give you and what can't it give you?

- CAN provide a sense of accomplishment and significance, a good reputation
- CANNOT provide an ongoing thrill, result in others loving us, grant eternal life
    - Can achievement ever be enough?

6. How about appearance? If you could look like anyone, whom would you choose?

LEADER: If someone says, "I am happy just looking like myself," you might say **That's great! But is there anything at all you would like to change about yourself?** If the person still says "Nothing," just reply, **Good for you,** and move on to someone else. Again, don't argue, contradict, or try to make the participant give the answer you want.

*7. So, in your experience, what can appearance do for you and what can't it do for you?

- CAN make you popular, get you jobs and dates, cause others to admire or envy you

- CANNOT make someone love you, guarantee a happy marriage or happiness itself

    *8. How about relationships? What have you found that they can do for you and what can't they do for you?

- CAN make us feel deeply loved, special, wanted; provide a sense of community
- CANNOT last forever (people die or leave); satisfy that deepest part of us

    *9. On page 25 of your participant's guide, you'll see the words of Jeremiah that were quoted in the presentation.

> "My people have done two evils:
> They have turned away from me,
> the spring of living water.
> And they have dug their own wells,
> which are broken wells that cannot hold water."
> —JEREMIAH 2:13, NCV

Are our wells really broken?

a. Alfred Adler (psychologist and author) said that everyone needs purpose. What if a person had it all—lots of possessions, great achievements, good looks, and meaningful relationships? Is that enough to provide all the purpose someone would need in life?

b. What about the security Carl Jung (pychologist and anthropologist) said we all need? If we had it all, would that supply all the security we would want?

c. Sigmund Freud (originator of psychoanalysis) said we need love. Would having it all deliver all the love that a human being could ever need?

*10. The purposes Jesus offers us are to know God and live with Him forever as well as to participate in the mission of helping others know God and live with Him forever. How would you compare those purposes with the usual purposes people pursue in life, such as getting rich, raising happy kids, building a big company, or even finding a cure for cancer?

*11. How about the security Jesus offers? He says He can guarantee that those who come to Him will never perish, that He can grant them eternal life. Do you think that there is life after death, and if so, what do you think it is like?

- What do you think of Jesus' offer to give ongoing life?

*12. It was also claimed that Jesus offers unconditional love, that is, that He loves everyone regardless of what they are like. I don't think this means He approves of everything people do, but He cares deeply for them even when He doesn't like what they do. How does this compare to the kind of love you have experienced in the world?

*13. Jesus claims to offer living water, pure water. Based on what you know at this point, how would you describe what He is offering?

[ ] radiator fluid: it's actually poison, the opiate of the people

[ ] placebo water: it makes people think they are getting better but it's just a mirage

[ ] tonic water: it helps; it is good but not necessarily better than other drinks

[ ] living water: it's the only "good stuff" that can satisfy the deepest thirst

As each person answers, if they don't explain why they think that way, ask them to elaborate.

WRAP UP

It's about time to finish up. I really appreciate everyone being here.

- **A couple of things I found very interesting were . . .** Sum up some of the key insights of the evening as you see them.

- **Don't forget the "For Reflection" section.**

- Next week, I'd like you to bring a Bible if you have one. If you don't, no worries; I'll have extras.
  - OR, The next time we meet will be our overnight getaway. Here's _____ to give us all the details.
- Would someone like to close our night with a brief prayer? It doesn't have to be elaborate, just thank God or ask Him for what you want. If no one volunteers, then lead in a brief prayer yourself.

◀ FOR REFLECTION

"If I only had . . . , then I'd be happy!" How would you complete that sentence? If you only had a mate? If you only had a boatload of money? If you could only find the right career? Or maybe it's something as simple as "If I could only get the house cleaned up, the checkbook straightened out, and the kids to school on time!" How would you finish the sentence?

> "If I only had . . .
>
> then I'd be happy!

Is what you are pursuing in an effort to make yourself happy poisoning your life in some way? For example, you might be pursuing corporate success, but it is leading to ulcers and a shaky marriage. Or you might be going from one sexual relationship to another, but this is causing emptiness and regret. Identify any damaging effects to which your efforts to quench your thirst are leading.

Here are some Scriptures that are referred to in the DVD presentation. Circle anything that stands out to you.

> The words of the Teacher, son of David, king in Jerusalem:
> "Meaningless! Meaningless!" says the Teacher.
> "Utterly meaningless! Everything is meaningless."
>
> What does man gain from all his labor at which he toils under the sun?
> All things are wearisome, more than one can say.
> The eye never has enough of seeing, nor the ear its fill of hearing.
> —ECCLESIASTES 1:1–3, 8
>
> I thought in my heart, "Come now, I will test you with pleasure to find out what is good." But that also proved to be meaningless. "Laughter," I said, "is foolish. And what does pleasure accomplish?" I tried cheering myself with wine, and embracing folly—my mind still guiding me with wisdom. I wanted to see what was worthwhile for men to do under heaven during the few days of their lives.
>
> I undertook great projects: I built houses for myself and planted vineyards. I made gardens and parks and planted all kinds of fruit trees in them. I made reservoirs to water groves of flourishing trees. I bought male and female slaves and had other slaves who were born in my house. I also owned more herds and flocks than anyone in Jerusalem before me. I amassed silver and gold for myself, and the treasure of kings and provinces. I acquired men and women singers, and a harem as well—the delights of the heart of man. I became greater by far than anyone in Jerusalem before me. In all this my wisdom stayed with me.
>
> I denied myself nothing my eyes desired;
> I refused my heart no pleasure.
> My heart took delight in all my work,
> and this was the reward for all my labor.

*Yet when I surveyed all that my hands had done
and what I had toiled to achieve,
everything was meaningless, a chasing after the wind;
nothing was gained under the sun.* —ECCLESIASTES 2:1–11

Can anything ever separate us from Christ's love? Does it mean he no longer loves us if we have trouble or calamity, or are persecuted, or are hungry or cold or in danger or threatened with death? (Even the Scriptures say, "For your sake we are killed every day; we are being slaughtered like sheep.") No, despite all these things, overwhelming victory is ours through Christ, who loved us.

And I am convinced that nothing can ever separate us from his love. Death can't, and life can't. The angels can't, and the demons can't. Our fears for today, our worries about tomorrow, and even the powers of hell can't keep God's love away. Whether we are high above the sky or in the deepest ocean, nothing in all creation will ever be able to separate us from the love of God that is revealed in Christ Jesus our Lord. —ROMANS 8:35–39, *NLT*

The Spirit and the bride say, "Come!" And let him who hears say, "Come!" Whoever is thirsty, let him come; and whoever wishes, let him take the free gift of the water of life. —REVELATION 22:17

You may have tried talking to God before. Would you be willing to try writing your thoughts to Him? In a sense, it's just like writing a letter. Write what comes to mind. You may find it therapeutic.

**God,
Here are some of my thoughts. . . .**

LEADER'S GUIDE

Drowning

EPISODE 06

PURPOSE
- ❏ To unpack the cause of our troubles: sin

PREPARATION
- ❏ Prepare the meal.
- ❏ Set out name tags if needed.
- ❏ Cue DVD to Episode 06.
- ❏ Present a warm atmosphere with music, candles, etc.
- ❏ * Have extra Bibles available for participants who may not bring one.
- ❏ * All preparations completed for getaway

PRAYER
Lord, please . . .
- ❏ prepare participants' hearts to think honestly about sin
- ❏ convict us all of the ugly stuff we have inside

* designates new preparation items.

AFTER DINNER

Once you have gathered everyone to watch the DVD, ask:

> Our opening question this week is much tougher than some of the earlier ones. Here goes: Why is the world so messed up?

VIEW EPISODE 06 ▶ DROWNING

DISCUSSION

*1. What are your feelings after watching this segment?

*2. Has anyone ever paid your tab or saved you from a mess you couldn't get yourself out of? If so, what was that like for you?
- How did you find yourself responding to their efforts?

3. How about the other way around? Have you ever offered to foot the bill for someone who didn't deserve it or pull somebody's fat out of the fire when you didn't have to? If so, what did you do and why did you do it?
   - How did the other person respond?
   - How did you want him or her to respond?

*4. What do you think the chances are that God would do something like that for people on earth?

*5. Kyle brought up the dreadful Bible word: *sin.* Do you believe there is such a thing as sin, that is, real wrongdoing?
   - If people answer in the affirmative, say, **Kyle paraphrased sin as "When we do something we know is wrong or don't do something we know is right." How would you define wrongdoing?**
   - If people say there is no such thing as wrong, that it's all relative or simply social convention, then ask, **So would you say that nothing is ever really wrong, not murder, rape, bigotry, the Holocaust?**

   After they have had a chance to respond, ask, **What do the rest of you think about that?**

6. If there is such a thing as sin, do you think there is also some sort of "bar tab" or karma for everything people do wrong? I mean, is there some kind of payday for the sins people commit?

*7. Kyle mentioned four ways people deal with their ugly stuff, their sin.
   - One is to *deny* it, to just not face it.
   - Another is to *rationalize* it away. They say things like "I have a right to be happy; I'm not hurting anybody; I couldn't help it." Someone said that when we rationalize, we are actually telling ourselves "rational lies."
   - Another is to *compare* themselves with those who are worse—"At least I'm not as bad as so-and-so!"
   - The last is that people try to *hide* their bad habits—they stash their drug paraphernalia or never tell anyone the hateful thoughts in their heads.

   Do you think Kyle is right? If so, why do people do these things?

*8. One of the big questions about Christianity is why God would allow a Hell. If a person rebelled against God, wouldn't submit to God, what do you think God should do with such a person? Possible answers can be found on page 29 of your participant's guide.

- Let him into Heaven anyway (but then God would be letting sin into His perfection and immediately polluting it).
- Force this person to surrender (but this would violate his free will, robbing him of his right to choose).
- Give the person his wish (but this would mean separation from God and all that is good, that is, existence in outer darkness, or Hell).
- Create a nice place where sinful, unsubmissive people could go and continue to be sinful and unsubmissive but be as happy as they can be in this state (but this would violate God's justice and be unfair to those who had gone all out to do what was right).
- Just annihilate him (but then he wouldn't pay for the wrongs he did commit; people could literally "get away with murder").

*9. What did you think of the illustration of the two glasses of water? What do you think God should do with the dark stuff in people's cups?

*10. Tonight I would like for us to actually open up the Bible. If you don't have one, I have extras here. Hand out Bibles. **This is such an important section that I want us to see directly what the Bible says. Turn to Luke 23:33.** Help those who need it. **That's in the New Testament, or about two-thirds of the way in. That's on page _____ in the Bibles I handed out. Luke 23:33. If someone would be willing to read aloud this fairly long section, I would appreciate it. We'll read from verse 33 to verse 47. This is one of the records of Jesus' death. Thank you, _____, for reading. Let's all follow along.**

After the passage is read, **What stands out to you from this reading?**

What we just read tells what happened to Jesus. But why did it happen? Turn to Mark 10:45. Mark comes before Luke, the book that we just looked at. Mark 10:45. That's on page _____ in the Bibles I handed out.

Give everyone time to find the verse.

Jesus is speaking. He's presenting a kind of mission statement for His life. Would someone be willing to read this verse out loud? Thank you, _____.

Thanks again for reading.

Some of you may have been following along in a Bible with different words than what was just read. Just a word about why there are different versions of the Bible. The New Testament was written in Greek, so it has to be translated into English. There are lots of translations; some are strict, literal translations that focus on the meaning of the original words. Others are a bit freer and paraphrase the meaning in modern English. Here is a translation that might help make the meaning clearer:

Even the Son of Man did not come to be served.
Instead, he came to serve others.
He came to give his life as the price
for setting many people free." —MARK 10:45, *NIRV*

When Jesus uses the title "Son of Man," He is referring to himself. So what stands out to you from this verse?

*11. **Let's turn to one other place in the Bible, Isaiah. To find Isaiah, open up your Bibles halfway, and then go a little bit to the right and you'll find it. Then go to chapter 53. This is on page _____ in the Bibles I handed out. Again, that's Isaiah 53.**

Give people time to find it.

What we are going to read is a prophecy, a sort of advance notification from God about what He was going to do in the future. This was written about 700 years before Jesus' time. But it describes what Jesus would do. Would someone read verses 4–6? Thank you!

Again, in your participant's guide on page 30 is the same passage in the *New International Reader's Version.* Let's look at that.

He suffered the things we should have suffered.
   He took on himself the pain that should have been ours.
But we thought God was punishing him.
   We thought God was wounding him and making him suffer.

But the servant was pierced because we had sinned.
   He was crushed because we had done what was evil.
He was punished to make us whole again.
   His wounds have healed us.

All of us are like sheep.
   We have wandered away from God.
All of us have turned to our own way.
   And the Lord has placed on his servant
the sins of all of us. —ISAIAH 53:4–6, *NIRV*

What do you think of this idea of Jesus giving His life to pay the tab for our messing up?

WRAP UP

OVERNIGHT GETAWAY OPTION

This has been another fascinating night. Before we close

- **Let me just tell you that we are going to give you some time to do the "For Reflection" section tomorrow morning if you want to. So for those of you who are really conscientious, don't worry about it tonight.**
- **We have some snacks and drinks.**
- **Let me pray, and then we'll see you at breakfast at 8:30 in the morning.** See prayer on next page.

After breakfast, prepare for each participant both a glass half filled with clean water and a cup of black coffee, or some other dark-color drink. Gather everyone and say,

- **I hope you slept well and had a good breakfast.**
- **Before we view our next segment, I'd like to have you take some time to think through the "For Reflection" section from last night's session. This "For Reflection" section may be the most difficult part of the whole series, but I hope you will try it. I think it will be very worthwhile and for some of you eye-opening.**
- **I hope you'll find someplace alone—you can take a walk, go to your room, find a corner somewhere, but get away from everyone else.**

- You have from now until 10:30. The reflection won't take that long to complete, so feel free to take a walk as well. The one request I have is that you spend this time alone and in silence until 10:30.
- Any questions?

NON-OVERNIGHT GETAWAY OPTION

This has been another fascinating night. Before we close

- I want to strongly suggest you do the "For Reflection" section this week. You will need to find a time you can be alone and undisturbed for a while, maybe 30 minutes or even a little longer. It is a challenging section but one I think will be very much worth your while. If you do complete it, I'd like you to bring the glass it discusses with you next week. You'll understand what I mean when you do it. Again, you don't have to, but you might be glad you did.
- Now I'd like to end our evening together with a prayer.

Lord, I'm stunned by the idea that you would somehow pay for the ugly, selfish things I've done. But I am grateful. Would you help each of us to see how much we have messed up. Help us not to cover it up or rationalize it. And help us to see that you really do want to bail us out. Amen.

◄◄ FOR REFLECTION

What we suggest here may be difficult. But to get an honest assessment of your situation, you might decide to try it despite the difficulty.

To make the most of this time, have a glass half filled with clean water, and a cup of black coffee, cola, or some other dark drink.

Make a list of the bad stuff you've done. Think about different stages of your life—childhood, high school, college, your young adult years, and so on. Write down whatever unkind, selfish, or harmful things that strike you. It may be as "small" as teasing the neighborhood nerd or stealing pocket change from your mom's purse. It may be as "big" as getting your girlfriend pregnant or screaming profanities at your kids. Take your time. Don't rush. You won't have to show this page to anyone. So whatever comes to mind, write it down.

James 4:17 says, "Well, remember if a man knows what is right and fails to do it, his failure is real sin" (J. B. Phillips, *Translation of the New Testament, The New Testament in Modern English*). If this is true, then what "failure-sins" would you have to add to your list? What should you have done in each stage of life, but didn't? Helped your mom more? Been nice to the neighborhood nerd? Volunteered your time for some worthy cause? Spent time building up your kids? Again, take your time. Mull over things you knew you should have done but neglected.

How do you feel about your list? What is your reaction?

_____
_____
_____
_____

If a person did something wrong just five times a day—(tell a white lie, gossip about a coworker, blow up at the kids, ignore the nudge to do something good like call mom or encourage a friend)—in fifty years this person would have accumulated more than 90,000 offenses!

Would you guess your average number of shortcomings a day to be less than or more than five?

[ ] less than five   [ ] more than five   [ ] way more than five!

Take your glass of clean water. Add to it the amount of coffee or cola that you think represents how much bad stuff you have done in your life. Try to be honest. (If you're not honest, then you have to add dishonesty to your list too!)

So, how dark is your cup?

What will you do with the dark stuff inside?

Look back over the Scriptures that were read during the discussion (Luke 23:33–47; Mark 10:45; Isaiah 53:4–6). What are these passages saying to you now?

Keep your glass and its contents as a visual reminder until our next session. If you are willing, bring it with you to the next gathering.

Drink

PURPOSE
- To describe how a person can drink from the water of life
- To invite those who are ready to "exchange their glasses" and drink

PREPARATION
- Prepare for dinner.
- Set out name tags if needed.
- Cue DVD to Episode 07.
- Present a warm atmosphere with music, candles, etc.
- * Have pens ready for everyone.
- * Have extra glasses and cups of coffee (or cola or other dark beverage) for those who want to re-create their glass from the "For Reflection."
- * Set up a table in this way:
  Locate or make a cross.
  Set up the cross on an end table or, if it's large, on the floor.
  Place at the base of the cross a clean glass of water for each group member.
- * Cue DVD that contains the song "Amazing Grace." Have the DVD player near you or a team member so it can be turned on immediately at the appropriate time.
- * Inform team members in advance of the glass exchange and encourage them to participate as God leads. You might want to suggest that one or two of the team not bring their glasses with them but instead prepare a glass when you suggest it after dinner, in order to help others feel comfortable doing so as well. Also inform team members that the group will be singing "Amazing Grace" together. Encourage them to sing out.

PRAYER
Lord, please . . .
- make clear to everyone in this group the forgiveness and new life You are offering through Jesus
- motivate those who have not yet accepted Your clean cup to do so
- reenergize those who have lost the joy of Your gift

* designates new preparation items.

AFTER DINNER

(or after breakfast, if using the retreat format)

As you are gathering everyone for the DVD, suggest:

> If you didn't bring your glass from the "For Reflection" time, you can re-create one using the glasses and coffee cups I have over here. These glasses represent our lives. If you didn't do the reflection, then you need to know, we were encouraged to think through how much dark stuff we've put into our own glasses with the wrong things we've done. So we added that much coffee or cola to our glasses to represent that. Even if you didn't do the reflection, you can make up a glass if you want. As always, you don't have to do it, but it might be powerful for you. It's up to you. But I want you to know that we will interact with glasses during the session.

Give participants time to prepare their glasses. Then once you have gathered everyone to watch the DVD, ask:

> What's your favorite drink and what do you like about it?

VIEW EPISODE 07 ▶ DRINK

DISCUSSION

1. **Please turn to page 33 in your participant's guide. Before we discuss this presentation, would you jot down your responses to the questions on that page? I have pens here if anybody needs one.** Give them plenty of time to write their answers. Model what you want by honestly writing your own answers in the space provided.

Questions in the participant's guide:

- What are your thoughts and feelings after watching this segment?

- What questions do you have?

- Which is closest to how you have responded to God's free offer of a pardon and new life?

    - I don't believe it.
    - I don't need it.
    - I'll try to earn it.
    - I don't understand it.
    - I don't want it.
    - I'll simply accept it.

Put your response to what Jesus is offering in your own words.

2. **What are your thoughts and feelings after watching this episode?**

3. **What questions do you have?**

4. As questions arise, ask the group, **What are your thoughts about _____'s question?**

5. **As always, you don't have to speak up, but I'd be interested in hearing how each of you is responding to this offer of a new life.**

You need to be ready for anything, including individuals saying they prayed with Kyle. This next section is to be used if anyone has decided to receive Christ's pardon. If several respond, use this in the group. If only one or two accept, then you might talk through this section after the group meeting.

OPTIONAL SECTION

I just want to say that I'm extremely happy for you.

Did anyone else pray along with Kyle? If yes, *Wow, that's great!*

Would it be OK if I prayed for those of you who have decided to accept Christ's offer? If anyone agrees, pray a brief, simple prayer like,

Father in Heaven, how thrilled we are that _____ has decided to accept the free gift You offer through Jesus. We know You love them

and want the very best for them. We ask You to give them insight to understand your free gift, a heart to know You, and strength to keep following You even when it is hard. May they enjoy Your forgiveness and presence all the days of their lives and then live with You forever. In Jesus' name, amen.

In Kyle's prayer, he mentioned several ways to express new faith in Jesus. You may want to encourage group members to see what the Bible says about expressing faith in Jesus. Some may want to find the words on their own in a Bible concordance. A few sample verses are listed below.

a. Reject your old way of thinking and acting that was outside God's will. You see your old ways as wrong and decide to do things God's way as best you can. Nobody can do this perfectly, but you decide to try. The Bible calls this *repentance* (Acts 3:19, 17:30, 26:20).

b. *Confession* is simply saying aloud that you believe Jesus is Lord. (Matthew 10:32; Romans 10:9, 10; 1 Timothy 6:12–14). In a sense, confession is what you just did when you told this group that you decided to trust Jesus.

c. *Baptism* is when a person is dipped under water. It is a picture of dying to your old self, of burying your past, being totally cleansed of all your guilt, and being raised up to a new kind of life (Romans 6:3, 4; Galatians 3:26, 27; 1 Peter 3:20–22). Back when Jesus' first followers were around and the New Testament was being written, a person was always baptized soon after he or she decided to trust Jesus (Acts 2:40, 41; 8:26–40; 16:16–30). For those of you who accepted Christ's pardon, I'll meet with you after our group time to guide you into being baptized right away.

Does it make sense how these steps can help a person latch onto, or unwrap, God's free gift of salvation?

6. For those of you who already have or even just now accepted the pardon and new life Jesus offers, then I'd like to suggest one other thing. Now this isn't in the Bible, but it is in the spirit of the Scripture and it could be a neat thing to help you solidify your new life in Christ. In a moment I will give you an opportunity to exchange your dirty glass of water for a fresh one under the cross. You don't have to, but it might be a great symbol of what you are doing with your life. I'll tell you what—this will

be a stretch—but I'm going to play a rendition of "Amazing Grace" on the DVD player. If you would like, sing along. You don't have to sing if you don't want to, but the words are printed in your participant's guide on page 34. And while we are singing, if anyone wants to go and exchange your glass, feel free to do so.

Play DVD of "Amazing Grace." Help begin the singing. Then, if necessary, take the lead in exchanging your glass at the cross.

Amazing grace! How sweet the sound
That saved a wretch like me!
I once was lost, but now I'm found;
Was blind, but now I see.

'Twas grace that taught my heart to fear,
And grace my fear relieved;
How precious did that grace appear
The hour I first believed!

Through many dangers, toils and snares,
I have already come;
'Tis grace hath brought me safe thus far,
And grace will lead me home.

When we've been there ten thousand years,
Bright shining as the sun,
We've no less days to sing God's praise
Than when we'd first begun. —JOHN NEWTON, 1779

7. After the song, ask, **For those of you who exchanged your glasses at the cross, how did that feel? What was your reaction?**

8. **I'm going to leave the glasses up here for the rest of the retreat/night. If anyone else would like to exchange his or her glass, the cross and glasses will still be here.**

WRAP UP

- Before we close, since we did so well on "Amazing Grace," how about we try a few lines of the "Hallelujah Chorus," in Latin? No? OK, maybe next week!

- The next time we meet we will talk about what happens to

a person as a result of accepting this offer. I think it will be really meaningful.
- Don't forget the "For Reflection" section. It is a great way of processing our retreat/this episode.
- If anyone wants to talk further, I'll be glad to listen or pray with you—whatever you need.
- Close with a brief prayer.

◀◀ FOR REFLECTION

Some H20 groups go on an overnight getaway and complete Episodes 06 and 07. So the first three questions are especially geared for those who did. If your group didn't go away, just start with question four.

1. What was the time away like for you? How did you find yourself responding?

2. Are you satisfied with your response during the getaway, or do you wish it had been different? If different, in what way?

3. Do you have a sense that you met God or interacted with Him in some way during the time away? If so, what was that like? What did you make of it?

4. Where do you see yourself going next in your spiritual journey?

5. If you are not ready to accept Jesus' free offer of forgiveness of sins and escape from the death penalty, what's the reason?

   ____ I don't think the offer is real.

   ____ I don't need the help; I'm not that bad.

_____ I refuse to accept anyone's charity; I should pay for my own mistakes.

_____ I just feel too guilty to believe that I can ever be released from my guilt.

_____ I know I can't live up to it; I'll end up going back to my old ways

_____ Other: _____

6. The following passages of Scripture have been paraphrased for this exercise. They describe what Jesus has done for us and what it means for us. Personalize them by writing your name in each of the blanks.

> When they came to the place called the Skull,
> there they crucified him, along with the criminals
> —one on his right, the other on his left.
> Jesus said, "Father, forgive _____,
> for _____ does not know
> what he or she is doing." —LUKE 23:33, 34

> "For God so loved _____
> that he gave his one and only Son,
> that if _____ believes in him
> _____ shall not perish
> but have eternal life." —JOHN 3:16

> God saved _____ by his special favor
> when _____ believed.
> And _____ can't take credit for this;
> it is a gift from God.
> Salvation is not a reward for the good things _____ has done,
> so none of us including _____ can boast about it.
> For _____ is God's masterpiece.
> He has created _____ anew in Christ Jesus,
> so that _____ can do the good things
> he planned for _____ long ago. —EPHESIANS 2:8–10, NLT

> Christ never sinned but God put _____'s sin on Him.

> Then _____ is made right with God because of what Christ has done for _____. —2 CORINTHIANS 5:21, NLV

Try reading these passages aloud with your name in them. What is that like?

If you would like to find out what happened after Jesus' death, read Luke 24.

LEADER'S GUIDE

Clean

EPISODE **08**

PURPOSE
- ❏ To present three key, new identities believers have in Christ
- ❏ To show that the Christian life means living out these identities, not following a list of do's and do not's

PREPARATION
- ❏ Be sure to have dinner ready before participants arrive.
- ❏ Set out name tags, if needed.
- ❏ Cue DVD to Episode 08.
- ❏ Present a warm atmosphere.
- ❏ * Have extra pens.

PRAYER
Lord, please . . .
- ❏ protect from evil those who have recently trusted You
- ❏ influence everyone in this group to receive Your free gift
- ❏ make clear to each person these new identities You give us

AFTER DINNER

Once you have gathered everyone to watch the DVD, say,

> 1. **To begin, please take out your participant's guide and turn to page 37. I promise, no singing!**

Allow everyone time to turn there.

> **When someone asks, Who are you? how do you describe yourself? "I am . . . what?" Just write your answer in the big box. If you need a pen, I have some here.**
>
> 2. **Here's a tough question. Of the things you wrote down, which reveal you at your very core, and which are things that you simply do. For example, you may have said, "I'm a person, a human being." That is something you are at your core. But you might have said, "I'm an assembly-line worker." That is not something you are at your core but something you happen to do. But you might have written, "I'm Mr. Fix-it." That is something you are, whether you are fixing something**

or not. It's part of your nature. Does that make sense? Circle the things that you would say are at your core, part of your very nature.

LEADER: You may want to give examples from your own life rather than those above.

3. If you don't mind, tell us some aspect of your nature and how you came to have this at your center. I mean, were you just born with artistic ability or did you develop it? Did somebody build your self-discipline, such as a parent or a coach, or did you always have it?

4. Choose one of your identities and tell us how having that identity affects the way you live. For example, one of my core identities is that I'm a problem solver. I just love to figure things out. So I'm always tinkering with stuff.

LEADER: Feel free to give your own personal example.

That's all very interesting, and it will tie into tonight's episode! Let's watch.

VIEW EPISODE 08 ▶ CLEAN

DISCUSSION

*1. What's your reaction to the idea that the Christian life is living out new, God-given identities rather than following a list of rules?

*2. What's the difference between someone trying to follow the rules and someone living out of a new nature?

3. If God really gives these new identities, what might keep someone from actually living out of them?

*4. Kyle discussed three identities that the heavenly Father gives to those who turn to Him. The first is *child*. This next question is very important. Have any of you men actually played "Pretty, Pretty Princess" and worn the earrings, necklace, and crown? Ok, just kidding.

Let's open our Bibles again and this time look up 1 John 3:1. It's near the back of your Bibles, just before Revelation. Would someone mind reading it?

How great is the love the Father has lavished on us, that we should be called children of God! And that is what we are!

If a person really believes he or she is a child of God, and accepts that as a core identity, what effect might it have on his or her life?

*5. **A second identity is *sojourner* or *traveler* in this world. One of Jesus' closest followers, a guy named Peter, wrote to his fellow believers: "Dear friends, I urge you, as aliens and strangers in the world, to . . ." (1 Peter 2:11). How would you finish that sentence?**

Turn back in your Bibles just a little ways to 1 Peter 2:11. Let's look at how Peter finished his own sentence. That's 1 Peter 2:11. Here's what Peter said:

"Dear friends, I urge you, as aliens and strangers in the world, to abstain from sinful desires, which war against your soul."

How does the way Peter finished his sentence line up with the way our group finished it?

*6. **A third identity is an athlete. Kyle quoted this passage but let's look it up anyway: 1 Corinthians 9:25. That's further back to the left. If you get to Romans or Acts, you've gone too far. That's 1 Corinthians 9:25. Would someone read it?**

Thanks!

*Everyone who competes in the games goes into strict training.
They do it to get a crown that will not last;
but we do it to get a crown that will last forever.*

Do we have any runners in the group, or does anyone work out?

- **What's your regimen?**
- **If you were to tell someone how to get started, what would you advise?**
- **So, would you advise training versus simply trying then?**

LEADER: If no one runs or works out, try other disciplines, like playing an instrument or investing in the stock market.

7. **How might a person begin training to follow Christ?**

8. Does living out of these identities exclude having any rules at all? Could a person do whatever he or she wanted as long as it was in line with his or her identity?

*9. Of the three images—child, traveler, and athlete—which do you connect with right away?

Which do you find hardest to relate to?

*10. If you saw yourself as these three things—child, traveler, athlete—what would change in your life?

Would that be a good change, a bad change, a scary change? How would you characterize it?

WRAP UP

It's good to have you all here again.

- By the way, did anyone add your name into the Scriptures in the "For Reflection" section last week? What was that like?

- Since we discussed the idea that God wants to make all of us His daughters and sons, I thought, instead of having just one person close in prayer, that we would just let anyone who wants to say something to the Father in Heaven. Here are the ground rules:

  - You can say whatever you have on your mind. Prayer is just like talking—it is talking to an invisible, spiritual person rather than a visible, physical one.

  - However, nothing long-winded. Just a sentence or two.

  - Just be sincere.

  - OK? I'll leave some open space. If you want to say something to God, go ahead. Then I'll close.

....

◀◀ FOR REFLECTION

After experiencing this session, how do you see yourself now? Who are you? What are you? What are your core identities?

For each identity that you listed, write beside it what that identity leads you to do or be. For example, if you listed "teacher," that might lead you to find students, prepare lessons, or keep on learning.

Are there any of these identities that you would like to be rid of? If so, which ones, and why?

How does someone receive these new identities that God gives? John 1:12, 13 describes how someone becomes a child of God, the first identity Kyle talked about. According to this passage, how does this happen?

> But to all who did accept him [Jesus] and believe in him
> he gave the right to become children of God.
> They did not become his children in any human way—
> by any human parents or human desire.
> They were born of God. —JOHN 1:12, 13, NCV

What's your last name? _____

How did you get this last name? _____

What, if anything, goes along with having this last name? For instance, maybe you are a Jones, and the Joneses always play a lot of sports, graduate from college, and make good in the business world. Or you are a Smith, and the Smiths love music, eat pasta, and laugh a lot. What goes along with your last name?

_____
_____
_____
_____

Have you lived out this family identity, pushed away from it, or maybe done a bit of both?

_____
_____
_____

Those who decide to trust what God has done through Jesus are automatically given the Father's name and become His children. It is not something we must *earn*, but it is something we must *learn*. We learn how to be the child of God we have become. What might it be like to live out of this family identity?

Will you accept this family identity?

Vapor

EPISODE 09

PURPOSE
- ❏ To introduce and discuss the person of the Holy Spirit

PREPARATION
- ❏ Assure the meal is ready.
- ❏ Set out name tags if needed.
- ❏ Cue DVD to Episode 09.
- ❏ Present a warm atmosphere.

PRAYER
Lord, please . . .
- ❏ reveal yourself through Your Holy Spirit to each person present
- ❏ fill each person with your Spirit so that he or she may glorify You

AFTER DINNER

Once you have gathered everyone to watch the DVD, ask,

> **How would you explain to someone who has never ridden a bike what it's like, without being able to actually put him on a bike and let him try?**
>
> **What about falling in love? How would you describe what that is like to someone who has never been in love before?**

LEADER: Listen for people to say "It's hard to describe; you just have to experience it," so you can later reiterate the comment during the discussion following the DVD.

> **Do you think people could really understand what it's like to ride a bike or fall in love if they have never experienced it themselves?**

VIEW EPISODE 09 ▶ VAPOR

DISCUSSION

> ***1. Before we get into a full discussion about any one topic, I'd like to give each person a chance to share his or her reaction to this week's**

presentation—whatever it might be. So everybody gets a chance to make a comment before anyone else responds. OK?

If there is silence before everyone has shared, you might ask, **Does anyone else want to voice what they are thinking or feeling?**

After the comments, you could simply take off on some of the comments, rather than using the questions below. It would go something like this:

- **Shane said that the Holy Spirit seems too elusive, too subjective, to really be certain of. What do the rest of you think?**
- **Janna felt like she's experienced this Spirit all her life but never put a label on it. Anyone else have that sense?**

If you don't feel comfortable leading the discussion this way, follow the questions below or do a mix of both.

*2. **One of the roles of the Holy Spirit is to comfort believers in times of trouble. Has anyone had such an experience of God's comfort? If you're willing, tell us about what it was like.**

*3. **How about God's Spirit teaching believers and acting as our moral compass—a kind of global positioning system. Has anyone experienced that?**

- **How can you know the difference between your own intuition and a nudge from the Spirit or between the voice of conscience and the leading of the Holy Spirit?**

Some possible answers:

- **Does it align with God's nature and Word?**
- **Does it lead us to be more like Jesus?**
- **Is it something I would tell myself, or is it something I wouldn't have thought of on my own?**

4. **Another aspect of the Holy Spirit's work is that He communicates for us in prayer. How does this truth give the believer assurance that his or her prayers are heard and understood by God the Father?**

*5. One big question to consider is "How does someone receive this Spirit and really utilize His power?" Let's look in the Bible. Open to Acts 2 and we'll begin by looking at Jesus' promise to His twelve special disciples called apostles. Acts is in the New Testament, the last third of the Bible. Acts comes right after Matthew, Mark, Luke, and John. Those books tell the story of Jesus. Then Acts tells the story of the early believers in Jesus. If you get to Romans or Corinthians, you've gone too far.

- The events in Acts take place after Jesus died on the cross. His apostles thought it was all over, but three days later they met Jesus alive. God had raised Him from the dead to confirm that Jesus was innocent and that He really was the Son of God. Now Jesus is about to leave them and return to Heaven. Look at Acts 1:4–9. Would someone mind reading this for the group?

- So Jesus promised the apostles they would receive power when the Spirit came. Acts 2 recounts the first time the Holy Spirit came upon/or filled the apostles. Because of this special gift, the apostles were able to preach in all the languages of the Jews who had gathered in Jerusalem for a holiday called Pentecost. When the crowd was confused about what they were witnessing, Peter stood and addressed them all. He told them what Jesus did for everyone—how He died and then rose from the dead. Now look at verse 37. Would someone read that?

When the people heard this,
they were cut to the heart and said to Peter
and the other apostles,
"Brothers, what shall we do?" —ACTS 2:37

I especially want us to see Peter's reply. Look at verse 38 and tell me how it says someone receives the Spirit.

"Repent and be baptized, every one of you,
in the name of Jesus Christ
for the forgiveness of your sins.
And you will receive the gift of the Holy Spirit. —ACTS 2:38

So who has the Spirit living in them?

Everyone who repents, turns to Christ, trusts Him, and follows in baptism.

6. If every believer in Jesus has the Spirit, then why don't they always feel His power, guidance, and comfort?

Possible answers:

- There is a difference between having the Holy Spirit and submitting to the Holy Spirit.
- Remember the illustration of the baby's hands. It can take time to learn the ways of the Spirit.
- 1 Thessalonians 5:19 says, "Do not put out the Spirit's fire"; the *King James Version* says, "Quench not the Spirit." Sometimes we do things to quench the Spirit, like ignoring Him, sinning, or doubting His reality.
- The Spirit is said to be like the wind that blows where and how it will (John 3:8). As the Holy Spirit works in the individual lives of Christians, the results may be very different.

WRAP UP

This was deep tonight. I've really been challenged. A couple of things before we close:

- Next week is our last week! Can you believe it? We'll be starting a new H20 group in _____ weeks. If you would like to be part of making that happen or would like to invite someone to be part of it, let me know.

- We'd also like to have a party two weeks from tonight to celebrate the successful conclusion of this group. You can invite friends or family, anyone you would like to introduce to H20.

- Tonight, let's close like we did last week. Anyone can pray, but you sure don't have to. Again, no long prayers, but if you'd like to say something to God, please do.

◄◄ FOR REFLECTION

What questions do you still have about the Holy Spirit?

Would you like to have the gift of the Holy Spirit? Why or why not?

What do you conclude about God's desire for us to have the Holy Spirit as you read these verses?

> *Would any of you who are fathers*
> *give your son a snake when he asks for a fish?*
> *Or would you give him a scorpion*
>   *when he asks for an egg?*
> *As bad as you are, you know how*
>   *to give good things to your children.*
> *How much more, then, will the Father in heaven*
> *give the Holy Spirit to those who ask him!* —LUKE 11:11–13, GNB

> *Therefore do not be foolish,*
> *but understand what the Lord's will is.*
> *Do not get drunk on wine,*
> *which leads to debauchery.*
> *Instead, be filled with the Spirit* —EPHESIANS 5:17, 18

What difference do you think the gift of the Spirit could make in your life?

How will you respond to the promise and the command Jesus makes in the passages above (on page 41 of the participant's guide)?

The DVD encouraged us to fill ourselves with the Word of God in order to be filled with the Spirit. To connect with the Spirit, it helps to have some knowledge of the Spirit. Take time this week to meditate on these Bible passages about the Spirit. Underline or circle ideas you want to remember, ask about, or test in your own life.

"God's Spirit gives new life."

> Jesus replied, "I tell you for certain that you must be born from above before you can see God's kingdom!" Nicodemus asked, "How can a grown man ever be born a second time?" Jesus answered: I tell you for certain that before you can get into God's kingdom, you must be born not only by water, but by the Spirit. Humans give life to their children. Yet only God's Spirit can change you into a child of God. Don't be surprised when I say that you must be born from above. Only God's Spirit gives new life. The Spirit is like the wind that blows wherever it wants to. You can hear the wind, but you don't know where it comes from or where it is going. —JOHN 3:3–8, CEV

The Holy Spirit causes "rivers of living water" to flow in the lives of believers.

> On the last day, the climax of the holidays, Jesus shouted to the crowds, "If anyone is thirsty, let him come to me and drink. For the Scriptures declare that rivers of living water shall flow from the inmost being of anyone who believes in me." (He was speaking of the Holy Spirit, who would be given to everyone believing in him; but the Spirit had not yet been given, because Jesus had not yet returned to his glory in heaven.) —JOHN 7:37–39, LB

The Spirit guides us to the truth.

> "I still have many things to tell you, but you can't handle them now. But when the Friend comes, the Spirit of the Truth, he will take you by the hand and guide you into all the truth there is. He won't draw attention to himself, but will make sense out of what is about to happen and, indeed, out of all that I have done and said. He will honor me; he will take from me and deliver it to you." —JOHN 16:12–14, THE MESSAGE

The Holy Spirit is a Counselor who lives within believers.

> *And I will ask the Father, and he will give you another Counselor to be with you forever—the Spirit of truth. The world cannot accept him, because it neither sees him nor knows him. But you know him, for he lives with you and will be in you. I will not leave you as orphans; I will come to you.* —JOHN 14:16–18

The Holy Spirit reminds Christians of Jesus' teachings.

> *I am telling you these things now while I am still with you. But when the Father sends the Counselor as my representative—and by the Counselor I mean the Holy Spirit—he will teach you everything and will remind you of everything I myself have told you. "I am leaving you with a gift—peace of mind and heart. And the peace I give isn't like the peace the world gives. So don't be troubled or afraid.* —JOHN 14:25–27, *NLT*

Those who repent and are baptized "receive the gift of the Holy Spirit."

> *When the people heard this [the truth about Jesus], they were cut to the heart and said to Peter and the other apostles, "Brothers, what shall we do?" Peter replied, "Repent and be baptized, every one of you, in the name of Jesus Christ for the forgiveness of your sins. And you will receive the gift of the Holy Spirit. The promise is for you and your children and for all who are far off—for all whom the Lord our God will call."* —ACTS 2:37–39

The Spirit reminds us "that we are God's children."

> *The Spirit himself testifies with our spirit that we are God's children.*
> —ROMANS 8:16

The Holy Spirit prays for us when we don't know how to pray.

> *And the Holy Spirit helps us in our distress. For we don't even know what we should pray for, nor how we should pray. But the Holy Spirit prays for us with groanings that cannot be expressed in words. And the Father who knows all hearts knows what the Spirit is saying, for the Spirit pleads for us believers in harmony with God's own will.* —ROMANS 8:26, 27, *NLT*

One day we will be raised to eternal life by God's Spirit.

> *You are no longer ruled by your desires, but by God's Spirit, who lives in you. People who don't have the Spirit of Christ in them don't belong to him. But Christ lives in you. So you are alive because God has accepted you, even though your bodies must die because of your sins. Yet God raised Jesus to life! God's Spirit now lives in you, and he will raise you to life by his Spirit.* —ROMANS 8:9–11, CEV

God's Spirit helps us to have those qualities that make us more like Jesus.

> *God's Spirit makes us loving, happy, peaceful, patient, kind, good, faithful, gentle, and self-controlled. There is no law against behaving in any of these ways. And because we belong to Christ Jesus, we have killed our selfish feelings and desires. God's Spirit has given us life, and so we should follow the Spirit.* —GALATIANS 5:22–25, CEV

> Don't forget to be thinking about whom you might like to invite to the H20 party. Or even better, ask the Spirit to bring to mind those you might ask and then give you the courage to ask them.

LEADER'S GUIDE

The River

EPISODE 10

PURPOSE
- To encourage participants to find a local body of believers where they can experience encouragement, teaching, and love
- To provide some pointers on finding such a group
- To allow everyone to reflect on what they gained from this series and what they plan to do next
- To promote the next H20 group

PREPARATION
- Prepare your "last supper."
- Set out name tags if needed.
- Cue DVD to Episode 10.
- Present a warm atmosphere.
- * Ask a team member to be ready to pray for you at the end of the session. Also have a couple team members ready to receive prayer "in the chair" (see "Wrap-Up").

PRAYER
Lord, please . . .
- help participants see the value of being connected to other believers
- show us how to continue the momentum of what You are doing in this group
- lead us all to invite others to the next H20 group

* designates new preparation items.

AFTER DINNER

Once you have gathered everyone to watch the DVD, ask,

- **What are some of your *least* favorite places to go, and why?**

Examples: in-law's house, dentist, shopping, hospital, work, church.

- **What are your *favorite* places to go, and why?**

VIEW EPISODE 10 ▶ THE RIVER

DISCUSSION

1. If you knew of a place to belong like Kyle described, would you be part of it? Why or why not?

   - Do you think it is possible that there are groups of people like that?

2. What's the best group you've ever been a part of—a ball team, club, maybe your own family?

   - What made it so good?
   - Was there anything bad about it? Any shortcomings?

3. No matter how good a group might be, there will also be some negatives. But in worthwhile groups, the good outweighs the bad. The DVD portrayed several nightmare versions of church. What would be your biggest fear of going to church?

   - Would it be worth facing this fear if you could find a place like Kyle described?

4. Let's open our Bibles to Acts 2. It's about two-thirds of the way through the Bible. Kyle referred to verses 42-47 throughout his presentation.

Give them time to find the passage.

One aspect of a healthy church is *no irrelevant teaching.* Look at Acts 2:42: "They devoted themselves to the apostles' teaching."

   - What makes teaching relevant, worthwhile, and meaningful?
   - Why would anyone go to a church where the teaching isn't relevant?
   - How would listening to uninteresting, unintelligible, or meaningless teaching week after week affect someone?

5. Another aspect of a healthy church is that no one stands alone. Notice verse 42 talks about fellowship, breaking bread—that's eating together and taking the Lord's Supper together—and prayer. Would someone read verse 46?

- Why do people try to stand alone in life?
- What happens to them when they do?
- How do you connect with others?

6. Another rule Kyle gave was that the church should be a place where *masks aren't worn.* Kyle noted the word *sincere* in verse 46. The early Christians were real.

    - What leads people to wear masks?
    - Would you really want to be a part of a group where the masks came off?
    - How could a person have enough courage to take off the mask?
    - What if a person really accepted the truth that he is a child of God—could he take off the mask then?

7. The fourth rule was *no part-time worship.* He pointed out the words *every day* in verse 46. How do you think people ever got to the place that they thought going to church on Sunday was all that was needed?

*8. The fifth rule was *no perfect people allowed, only changed people.* These people in Acts were doing a lot of good things—selling their possessions, helping the poor, praising God. But notice the last line of verse 47: "The Lord added to their number daily those who were being saved." It doesn't say they were perfect but that they were saved, being changed into what God really wanted. The church should be a place where people are growing and getting better.

    - Let me ask this: How have you been changed during this series?

*9. What's next for you on your spiritual journey?

    - If any of you would like to try attending a church, I'd like to invite you to go to church with me this weekend. It's not perfect, but I find it meaningful. Suggest a meeting place, perhaps offer to eat together afterwards (or even buy a meal for those who are not currently attending a church).

WRAP UP

This has really been a great series. Don't forget:

- Next week is our party to celebrate completing this series.
- This party is potluck—everybody bring something. We'll still have dinner, but I'm not cooking. It's your turn!
- Please invite friends—especially those who you would like to try the next H20.
- We will show an H20 preview, but there is no regular presentation or discussion. We'll explain to our guests that this is a party celebrating the end of H20 and invite them to the next session.
- Any questions?

CLOSE

- We've closed all our nights in prayer, which is fitting since we are trying to know God. Tonight I'd like us to pray for whoever wants to be prayed for. I am going to put a chair in the center of the room. Do so as you speak. I'd like the rest of us to gather around it.
- Then, if you would like us to pray for you, just sit down, and we'll say a brief prayer for you, for whatever you want. I'll go first.

Sit down in the chair and give a brief yet real request. Maybe you want energy to lead the next group or need wisdom for a problem at work.

- I would like _____ (whomever you asked in advance) to pray for me. If the rest of you would like to, just put a hand on my shoulder while he prays. It's a way of connecting and supporting me while _____ prays for me.

The person praying should be instructed in advance to say a brief prayer of thanks for you and a prayer for your request. Do not pray for anything but the request. That gives others the assurance that if they sit in the chair, you won't begin praying all kinds of things for them that they don't really want!

- Thank you! Now, as always, you don't have to do this! Only do it if you want to. But I've found there is great power in allowing others to pray for me. So if you would like to, we would be pleased to pray for you. You don't even have to share a request unless you want to.

Have a team member or two ready to be prayed for to help the others feel more comfortable.

When someone sits down, ask, **Is there anything you would like us to pray for you about? Who would you like to have pray for you? You can choose anyone as long as he or she is willing.**

Continue until everyone who wants prayer is prayed for.

- That's great. I'm glad to be part of such a special time.
- I look forward to next week and tasting YOUR food for a change!
- See you then!

◄◄ FOR REFLECTION

What is your overall response to H2O and its message?

What would you say you learned?

What did you decide during this course?

What questions do you still have?

Whom would you like to invite to the next H2O?

How about writing a prayer to God in response to this course? Say whatever you sincerely think or feel. Maybe add a prayer that those you invite to the next session of H2O would be open to trying it.

These Scriptures were mentioned in Episode 10.

Acts 2:42–47

They devoted themselves to the apostles' teaching and to the fellowship, to the breaking of bread and to prayer. Everyone was filled with awe, and many wonders and miraculous signs were done by the apostles. All the believers were together and had everything in common. Selling their possessions and goods, they gave to anyone as he had need. Every day they continued to meet together in the temple courts. They broke bread in their homes and ate together with glad and sincere hearts, praising God and enjoying the favor of all the people. And the Lord added to their number daily those who were being saved.

Matthew 7:28, 29

When Jesus had finished saying these things, the crowds were amazed at his teaching, because he taught as one who had authority, and not as their teachers of the law.

Hebrews 4:12

For the word of God is living and active. Sharper than any double-edged sword, it penetrates even to dividing soul and spirit, joints and marrow; it judges the thoughts and attitudes of the heart.

Galatians 5:13, 14

You, my brothers, were called to be free. But do not use your freedom to indulge the sinful nature; rather, serve one another in love. The entire law is summed up in a single command: "Love your neighbor as yourself."

1 Thessalonians 5:11

Therefore encourage one another and build each other up, just as in fact you are doing.

Romans 15:7

Accept one another, then, just as Christ accepted you, in order to bring praise to God.

Revelation 21:1–4

Then I saw a new heaven and a new earth, for the first heaven and the first earth had passed away, and there was no longer any sea. I saw the

Holy City, the new Jerusalem, coming down out of heaven from God, prepared as a bride beautifully dressed for her husband. And I heard a loud voice from the throne saying, "Now the dwelling of God is with men, and he will live with them. They will be his people, and God himself will be with them and be their God. He will wipe every tear from their eyes. There will be no more death or mourning or crying or pain, for the old order of things has passed away."

Revelation 22:1–5

Then the angel showed me the river of the water of life, as clear as crystal, flowing from the throne of God and of the Lamb down the middle of the great street of the city. On each side of the river stood the tree of life, bearing twelve crops of fruit, yielding its fruit every month. And the leaves of the tree are for the healing of the nations. No longer will there be any curse. The throne of God and of the Lamb will be in the city, and his servants will serve him. They will see his face, and his name will be on their foreheads. There will be no more night. They will not need the light of a lamp or the light of the sun, for the Lord God will give them light. And they will reign for ever and ever.

H2O Party

PURPOSE
- To celebrate the group's completion of H2O
- To provide a warm, accepting, comfortable setting
- To encourage guests to attend the next session of H2O

PREPARATION
- * Prepare invitation cards for the next session of H2O to hand out to guests.
- Ask two participants to be ready to share their experiences of H2O in two minutes or less. If it's a mixed group, you might want to choose one male and one female.
- Cue DVD to "H2O Preview"
- Present a warm atmosphere with music, candles, etc.
- Have plates, napkins, cups, and utensils available

PRAYER
Lord, please . . .
- move the participants to invite friends and family
- lead me about whom to ask to share a testimony of his or her experience with H2O
- give many a desire to attend the next session of H2O

* designates new preparation items

AT DINNER

- Have fun!

AFTER DINNER

- While everyone is enjoying dessert, gather everyone together.
  - Explain that the purpose of the party is to celebrate the completion of a DVD series called H2O and also to invite anyone interested to attend the next session of H2O.
  - Invite the two group members to share their experiences of H2O.

- Show the H20 preview.
- Inform everyone when the next series begins and hand out the invitation/information cards.
- Tell everyone that if they have questions, they can ask whoever invited them.
- Keep this gathering time brief, but welcome everyone to stay as long as they like.
- Begin forming your next H20 team from the participants in this H20 group.

What do you do with the difficult, domineering, excessively talkative participant? Try these ideas:

1. If someone is talking on and on, interrupt . . . nicely. Say "I see what you mean. Let's see how others feel about that."

2. If someone is regularly talking too much, you might say "I'd like to give everyone a chance to say one thing before anyone speaks a second time."

3. If someone continues to dominate, step aside with him or her after a session. Say something like "I see you have a lot of ideas and are willing to express them. That's great. But I need your help. Some of the others aren't so bold. Would you help me draw them out? How?"

4. To a person(s) who never talks, you might say "Does anyone who hasn't spoken up yet have a thought?" If that doesn't work and the Spirit seems to be prompting you, you might say "Kevin, I noticed you haven't said anything. I'd be interested in hearing what you think."

> **Above all, love each person in the group. If you truly care about them, they will sense it, and the Holy Spirit will flow through you!**

Helps for the OVERNIGHT GETAWAY COORDINATOR

The Overnight Getaway can be a powerful time of connection and decision. When people get away from the their usual haunts, they often can see life in a fresh way. Here are a few tips for the coordinator:

1. Find a suitable location.
   a. The best setting is someplace surrounded by nature so group members can take a walk or just drink in the beauty. God draws people to Him through His creation.
   b. Try Christian retreat centers, state park cabins, or rental condos. Maybe someone in the group or on the team has, or knows someone who has, a lake house or beach condo that would work.
   c. Keep the cost as low as possible for those who may not have a lot of extra money.
   d. Get accurate pricing to bring back to the group to avoid any surprises.
   e. Make sure your directions are clear and accurate. Give everyone the phone number of the place where you will be staying.
2. During the Overnight Getaway:
   a. Arrive early and make sure everything is as it should be.
   b. If the lodging does not have a TV and DVD player, arrange for them to be brought and set up. Be sure to try them out before the evening session begins.
   c. Take care of all the details as the home leader would: room setup, thermostat adjustment, prepare some snacks and drinks.
   d. Here's a sample Overnight Getaway timetable:

Friday

7:00 P.M.	Dinner
8:00 P.M.	View and discuss Episode 06.
9:15 P.M.	Snacks, hang out

Saturday

8:30 A.M.	Breakfast
9:15 A.M.	Encourage individuals to find a place alone and interact with the Reflection section from Episode 06.
10:30 A.M.	View and discuss Episode 07.
Noon	Lunch together
Afternoon	Return home or plan something fun to do together.

For the WHOLE TEAM

How do I invite someone?

Actually, asking people to come may be the most daunting part of this venture. But be encouraged. Once you get started, it gets easier. And usually you'll be surprised at who says yes. Here are a few keys:

- The most important thing you can do is to ask God to prepare the hearts of those you will invite.
- Most people do want connection and will be glad someone is interested in them.
- When inviting, avoid using the term Christianity. Instead, focus on Jesus. Rather than saying, "We're going to discuss what Christianity is all about," say, "We're going to look at who Jesus was and is."
- Do not trick people. Do not invite people for dinner, then spring the DVD on them. Be clear that you will watch and discuss a DVD about Jesus.
- To get you thinking, here are some suggestions on what you might say:
    - "Hey, there's a group of us getting together for dinner and to talk about spiritual things—would you be interested?"
    - "I'm going to a friend's house to watch a DVD talking about who Jesus really is. Would you consider going with me?"
    - "Have you heard about H2O? It's this really cool DVD that tells the truth about Jesus. We're going to discuss it over at _____'s house. We're also having dinner. I'd love for you to come."
    - "I think you are probably going to Hell since you are not a Christian, but I know this home group that can show you the light. What'll it be: learn or burn?" (OK, probably better not to use this last one.)
- If they say they'll think about it, contact them again later just to say "I hope you'll come. I think you'll like it, but if you don't like it, you don't have to go back. What do you have to lose?"

FINAL QUIZ

Jesus said in John 13:35, "By this all men will know that you are my disciples, if you . . ."

- a. know everything
- b. lead perfect lives
- c. win every argument
- d. have a clean house
- e. love each other

Besides inviting God's power into H20 through prayer, the most important factor in making this enterprise a success is actually caring about the people each of you invites. You can treat attenders in one of two ways: as projects or as people. This chart shows the difference:

PROJECTS	OR	PEOPLE
Someone to convince		Someone to care for
A goal, a target, an objective		A human, a name, an individual
A win/lose situation: either I win them to Christ or it was a waste		A win/win situation: even if they don't trust Jesus, I have shown them love and may have planted a seed for their future decision

The greatest commandment is not to win people to Christ but to love people regardless of how they respond to Christ. Paul made it clear that even if he were the greatest witness in the world but didn't have genuine love, his life would end up a big fat zero. So determine to love people. If you do that, no matter what else happens, you will have taken the most excellent way and become for someone else a taste of the living H20.